Let's Talk About Jesus

Joseph Haugabrook

This book is dedicated to my loving wife, Joann M. Haugabrook for her love, dedication and support

# Table Of Contents

PAGES

8. Let's Talk About Jesus
8. My Creed
9. Love: The greatest under-used asset given to mankind
11. General Information
17. Understanding God's Word
23. The reality of God's Word
27. It's important to know God's Word
28. There are basics that must be adhered to in living for God
33. Believe
34. Faith
36 . Prayer
38 . Forgiveness
39. Truth shall set you free
41. What's happening in the church?
43. A time of reflection
45. God didn't create the mess mankind is experiencing
46. God commandment to all living things to fill the earth with its kind.
51. The great gift from God
54. It is a gift from God
57. Be Fruitful and Multiply
63. Jesus Provides For His People
64. God's Word Will Get The Job Done
68. Why men make something, or someone, other than Jesus their god.
71. The source of wisdom
73. The Danger Of Man's Wisdom

78. Don't let your wisdom be a stumbling block
81. Isn't there a solution to the problems of the nations?
83. There is a solution to present day problems
86. People of God settling their differences among themselves.
90. Let nothing steal your God given joy
93. Don't worry about others; just trust in the Lord and do good.
95. What should I do? (Troubles)
99. Impatience
101. Train up a child in the way he should go
103. Lest we forget.
105. Think before you speak
107. Use your gift to further the works of God
109. Don't rejoice in other's calamity
111. Take note of the way you worship God
113. Bearing fruit in God
115. Be guided by God
117. The blessings of the Lord
120. Believe and trust in the Word
122. Believe what God says
125. Believe
127. Be faithful in all your dealings.
129. Living together in Christ
131. Truth will make you free
132. Love
135. Love covers all sins
138. Our relationship with Jesus
140. Don't be surprise at what the world do and say to you.
141. Why?
144. Don't forget who He is.
147. Trust in Jesus
149. The Lord is my shepherd
153. Your daily service

158. We never know who God is using or why

160. God hears us no matter what predicament we are in.

163. Powerful commandments of God

165. Words and actions without love

167. Make sure others see the light in you

169. Why men sin so easily

172. How is a person defiled?

175. Let the words of my mouth

177. A divided house

180. We are blessed

182. What you get for staying with Jesus; what you lose by leaving

185. When you pray

188. Easy and simple

191. Let not your heart be trouble

194. You will see it again

195. When you willingly accept Jesus

198. If Jesus was here

200. Walk in the light

203. Who do you believe Jesus is?

205. We are not perfect, just forgiven

207. Strong in your place of worship; weak outside

209. Denying Jesus

211. We can persecute Jesus by not knowing the truth.

213. One (you) can make a difference

216. Appreciate God's blessings

220. Measure your love by this

221. Life is not found in earthly possessions

224. First understand yourself

226. Should we be concerned about the end of the world?

228. Look closely at your reasons for seeking Jesus

231. How do we know we are walking in darkness?

234. Accepting Responsibility for our acts

236. Don't let anyone or anything stop you

239. The Great Invitation

240. Mustard seen faith

242. Power of the tongue

245. Resisting temptation

247. Don't ask; why me God; say; help me God

249. Loving your child to death

252. What are childish things?

255. Being unequally yoked with unbelievers

258. Vengeance was not assigned to man

259. Understanding Revelation

# LET'S TALK ABOUT JESUS

First and foremost; this book is you and I. I am talking directly to you about a relationship with Jesus Christ.

## My Creed

I understand that I cannot effectively express to others what I truly don't believe, practice and live. I must first possess what I desire to teach.

I will study the word to understand its purpose in my life and the lives of those I interact with.

I will strive, without exception, to be like Jesus; giving love and mercy to those I interact with.

I will not be moved from truth and reality by problems, perceptions and beliefs of man.

I believe and will teach others that Jesus Christ is our savior. His words, as recorded in the bible, are the answer to our problems and the problems plaguing mankind.

I have faith in Jesus Christ. I trust in His Holy Word. This I will show in words and deeds all the days of my life.

The world is a garden. Each of my life long deeds is a seed that I plant in my garden. Every seeds will sprout and produce fruit that I'll have to harvest. Only God knows them all, for there are some that I may have forgotten. My prayer is; Jesus, please destroy the bad ones I've planted and give me the knowledge, understanding and wisdom not to plant another one, not ordained by you.

I understand that whatever I do to my fellow man I'm doing to you. If I hate my fellow man, I hate you. If I turn a deaf ear to my fellow man, I'm turning a deaf ear to you. If I love and respect my fellow man, I love and respecting you.

Your written Word is your voice speaking to mankind. So, I will read it daily so I can hear your voice speaking to me.

I will speak your Words in bible class, Sunday school, general conversations in homes and communities; and, will live the Words I speak. This is my prayer and practice all the days of my life.

## LOVE

## The Greatest Under-Used Asset Given To Mankind

The church established by Jesus; is the pillar of righteousness, and moral strength. But, it's fast being separated into disagreeable units, resulting in confusion on an epic scale. The bible, which is the church's guide to daily living, and interacting with people, is being taught and used in a way that changes the real meaning to one that fits the thinking of those with agendas, contrary to truth and facts. Example: that which the word of God calls abomination, man has changed to be acceptable; citing "Politically correct" as the reason abominable acts can no longer be considered abominable. This is a division in the church; the last establishment of hope, that mankind looks to for righteousness, love, unity and peace among each other.

Look around you and ask your self this question: why are there wars among nations; is it because of unity? Why are there divorces and separation of families; is it because of love, understanding, cooperation, sharing, and caring for family members? Why is the moral strength of our nation being sapped at an alarming rate; is it because of love, understanding, cooperation, sharing, and caring offered to one another? And finally; why are elected offices, from the president to the local PTA being filled with those that can mount the greatest lying and mud slinging campaigns against his or her opponent?

Anytime facts are substituted by fiction; it's separation. And it doesn't matter who is providing the atmosphere of separation, the fact that it's provided is the important thing. The Pharisees were the experts of the law. These were groups that had the respect of the people looking for expert interpretations of the law. And they were the ones calling Jesus a devil. But, in reality who was the devil? It was the ones spreading lies about Jesus; in this case, the Pharisees. When we let so-called expert advice, replace the teachings of Jesus Christ, we are inserting division, confusion, frustration, misunderstanding and hatred into our thinking and practices. And this has the same effect as rot on wood; truth and facts, In our lives, are headed for total destruction.

10

# General Information

You have probably heard; I know I have, that the bible is confusing. But I hasten to add; the bible is not confusing, nor did God intend for his word to be confusing to anyone wanting to know his instructions on how to be obedient to his word in conducting their daily life in accordance with his Commandments.

God word is simple. It teaches how to interact with; people, places and things. Every lesson, or example given, focuses on how to interact with love and truth with those three things. It teaches how to apply truth and love in every situation encountered throughout life. However, before love and truth can be applied, both must be understood. Here is a clear understanding.

1. Let truth be truth: Don't try making something real; when it's not. Example: pretending: Saying something is right, knowing it is wrong. Or something is wrong; knowing it is right. If it's unknown; don't try putting a face on it. If it has a face, acknowledge what's there. If it's faceless, acknowledge that fact. Light is not darkness; darkness is not light. They are different, and, serve a different purpose; both beneficial; both good. So then, truth is; recognizing and accepting what's there without touching it up in any way.

2. Love; in its purest form is: wanting the very best for others and doing all you can to make it happen. Jesus demonstrated it through his actions toward mankind. He suffered the punishment for humanity's sins; was separated from the Father, died, went into hell, served the time for those sins, and is now on the Right Hand of God, still loving all mankind; saints and sinners. Jesus is the example for all mankind to follow. So, in interacting with each other daily,

Jesus example should be followed to the letter.  So, in reading the bible, don't read it to try an understand God, but to understand how to interact with the people, places and things encountered each day. Don't even read it to try and analyze the words and actions of others you interact with. Read it to note your responses (what to say and do) prior to any action; that is, think of a loving way to respond to a question, challenge, or giving advice.

The whole bible is the Word of God. But, since Jesus fulfilled the Old Testament, the New Testament is our guide for living Holy and righteous. So, although you are encouraged to read the Old Testament, which shows plainly how God dealt with mankind; their sins and righteousness; it is the New Testament that teaches how to live a life that pleases God in the time in which we live. Meaning; starting with Matthews, read all the way through Revelation. Read it, study it, follow it; let it shape your ideas, thought and control your actions and deeds. And never give a thought to the length of time it will take to read all the books, just focus on reading at least one chapter daily. Consistence reading gives a better understanding of how to use scripture in every instant of life.

God's Word can be compared to a good mechanic having every tool needed in his garage to do a good job on any kind of car brought into the shop. The bible provides every tool needed to handle any situation faced in life; in a kind, loving, caring and truthful way. But, it must be understood and properly applied. That's why it's so important to read the entire New Testament.  There is a danger in picking certain verses to read. Not fully understanding what is being said can lead to the bible being seen as contradicting itself; which can lead to arguments because it's being seen and understood in a different light. It causes some to believe that certain scriptures must be picked and applied to certain problems; and why that has merit; the wrong scripture can be picked and applied to the situation it's being thought to correct. Meaning; you are applying certain scriptures to a problem or condition without understanding how the word of God works, and how it is to be used. The mechanic may have many tools in his garage that look alike or seem right, but are not right for the job at hand. So he has to know what tool to use for the job. It is vital to understand each lesson in each book of the New Testament; how it teaches you to interact with people, places and things; because this is being obedient and serving God the way he commands us to. Every verse in the bible has a purpose, that's why it's important to read continually so the word will be fresh in your mind at all times. But, don't worry about which verse to use at any given time; because the Holy Ghost will bring to your remembrance the right one to use at the right time. That is; you will be given what to say, and how to say it, at the right time.

The Word of God is that powerful tool that can be used to accomplish any function needed in life. Note needed; because it is sometime believed that something is needed when in reality it's not. Example; think of a child going to his father and asking for something he believes he needs. The father, through wisdom and knowledge, know that the child neither needs what's being asked for, nor is it good for him. So he refuses. It may take time, maybe years, for the child to see that his father was right. In the mean time the child could have all kind of thoughts about the father's action; and could react in many ways. But, the father, acting out of love, does what he knows is best for his child. God always acts in the best interest of his children; that's why it's so important to be patience. I reiterate, God loves his children very much and knows what's best for them. He always acts out of love in answering the prayers and fulfilling the needs of his children. This is what's so wonderful about having a relationship with God. We, his children, have a Father that knows all things; good and bad. He knows how everything his children faces will fit into their lives. He knows, from birth how each of his children will act to that new car, house and everything he give them in life; and will never give anything that's going to harm their souls. Earthly parents will never give their child something they know will take their life, or harm them in some way. Much more with God, who knows all things. He doesn't give his children things that going to make them act in a way that will harm their soul. God want our soul saved to enjoy the things he has prepared for them; both in this life and in the life to come. Not understanding that can cause some to turn from God and find ways other than God's way to get things. Or, just turn from God's Word altogether; as some of Jesus followers did when they misunderstood his teachings of eating his flesh and drinking his blood. It is a joy for earthly parents to give to loving, obedient, respectful children. They will strive hard to give them the best things in life. God does much more for his loving, obedient, respectful children. Loving, obedient, respectful children learn what their parent's rules are and obey them. It's the same with God's children. God rules are spelled out plainly in His bible. Learn what God says about daily living. Treat people the way it says treat them. It's plain, simple and easy to understand. Never think God will hide the understanding of His Word. That's why He warns of adding or taking away from His Word as written. When something is added, or taken away, it creates confusion; causing some to misunderstand what's being said, or done. Making some feel there has to be more than what is written. So, they change it to what they think make more sense. Never do that! God Word is complete in itself. As stated above; God's Word will accomplish whatever is needed, when it's needed.

I hasten to add that God's Word is powerful and not to be toyed with. It can be compared to a large bundle of dynamite. The dynamic itself is very good and will do a good job if applied properly. It is also dangerous and will do grievous harm if handled improperly. The danger in God's Word is; using it to try and accomplish a selfish purpose. Example; win an argument; deceive another for the purpose of money, adultery, fornication, or to hide evil acts of any kind. The one committing such acts will find that what they are playing with will destroy them completely.

Look at it in reality. This world is a huge farm. Every male and female is a farmer. Every deed done is a seed planted on that farm. Every seed that's planted is going to sprout, grow and produce fruit. Every piece of fruit is going to be harvested, in this life; by the planter. The result of that harvest will be experienced in this life and the life to come. That is, the harvest will either be good fruit, resulting in good things on earth and eternal life; or bad fruit, resulting in evil things on earth and eternal damnation. The other thing is; harvesting the bad fruit is not going to be joyful. The same pains, feelings, hardships and other bad things resulting from the bad seed, will be experienced in the harvest. Galatians 6:7 are very clear on that. "Be no deceived; God is not mocked: for whatsoever a man soweth, that shall he also reap." God gives very clear direct instructions on how to use His Word. Just like the dynamite; Playing around with it is dangerous. Use it right and it will get the job done.

God will do wonderful things for his obedient children. But, his children must remember that God's plan is already laid out and he is not going to change it to fit our little selfish wants and desires. We, God's children, must

15

change to fit God's plan, not the other way around. That's why he explains plainly, that: first seek the Kingdom of Heaven. Understanding and obeying his Word is the first step in shaping our lives to His plan. That's done through a change in thinking beliefs and practices. Think spiritually about everything; every action and reaction. One of the easiest ways to exact change is to accept the fact that everything owned or possessed came from God. He is the giver of all good things. Thank Him for that drink of water that bite of food each breath; everything that sustain this life and his promises of eternal life. Once in the habit of thanking Him for everything, each day, you'll see a change in your life. And, the most beautiful part is; it will rub off on others.

Every human being owes it to Jesus to be obedient to his Word. Every human being owes love to one another. Everybody owes it to themselves to live this everyday. Remember; things that can be seen, felt and heard are the best teachers in the world.

# CHAPTER I

## Understanding God's Word

First, it must be understood that God didn't inspire the writing of his Word, the very thing he expects us to be obedient to, and live by, and then make it so confusing we wouldn't be able to understand it.

God's Word is given in a manner that provides a clear understanding of our roll on earth. How we are to speak, act and react toward one another. It shows what strength we have available through obedience, faith and belief. It shows how to think positive and use that positive thinking to gain an understanding of people and find solutions to problems, and ills of the world.

The Word should not be studied in an attempt to understand God. God is not telling us to try and understand him. He tells us to understand; first ourselves; why we act and react the way we do, then compare it to the standard He set for us to follow. God gives us enough for a clear understanding of how we are to conduct ourselves in the present; because we live in the present. Our words and deeds are done in the present. And during the instant we utter words, or commit deeds, we don't know or understand the full scope of God's programs for mankind. In this life, we will never fully know or understand God's whole program at any instant of time. Our minds just couldn't grasp its vastness. That is why in the 13th chapter of First Corinthians, he tells us plainly, we know in part, and we prophesy in part, which is telling us we understand, act and react in part, which is the reason why it is so important that our action coincide with what God tells us to do. These parts we act on are a part of the whole picture, and unless we act correctly our part will not fit into the whole picture. It's the same as putting together a puzzle; you can't take parts from one puzzle and fit them into another, especially different ones. We work on God's program piece by piece; and taking pieces from the world; (Satan's programs) and trying to fit them into God's program will never work; because God word shows clearly how to speak, act, and treat people in loving ways. God is saying (in his Holy Word) stop; look at your actions; your feelings; your thinking, and compare them with the outline I've given you to follow. In other words, look at your actions; the way you think; the way you react to situations; your morals and deeds; and overlay them with the word of God and see how far off you are. Anything that doesn't fit the overlay needs to be discarded and replaced with things that do fit. Example: hating another person, no matter the rationale, will never fit into God's program. Adultery, fornication, lying, cheating, deception, negative communication and much more, will not fit. God's word is transparent and the fit can easily be seen when we compare words and deeds. It's like chopping off your index finger then taking your thumb and trying to replace it. The misfit is quite obvious.

God made His program very easy to learn and follow. Under the New Covenant, Jesus made obedience to his word very plain. In John 13:34 He tells us how it's done. It simply requires that we love one another, the way he loved us. And note, His example was given of Him being in the flesh as you and I; being subjected to every temptation as you and I. He loved us enough to take on our sins, suffer the punishment of them, including dying and going into hell, separating Him for awhile from the Father; a suffering we couldn't begin to understand. Yet, through it all His thinking, words and deeds were an exact match to the Word of God. In other Words, his words and deeds fit the program of God perfectly.

When it comes to serving God, Jesus shows us exactly how God views our service to Him. In Matthews 25:34-45 He explains it this way; whatever you do to the least of your brethren you are doing it to me. In other words, when you love everybody without exceptions you also love God and are accepting the sacrifice Jesus made for us all. So, there is no way you can love God and hate other human beings. You may hate their evil deeds but it's the deeds, not the person; which is why when it's done this way you will work to change the thinking, actions, reaction and deeds of that person. I'm sure you've heard the old saying; I love the person but hate his or her deeds. God hate sins which we all are guilty of, but he love every one of us and make His blessings available to us all. So to serve God in the fullest, serve your fellow man in love and truth. Don't react to a person based on physical features or characteristic, but let your response be based on your knowledge, strength and faith in Jesus. It is important to remember at all times, that you must not let a situation control your actions; you must control the situation. When you let a person place or thing dictate your action, that thing is controlling you. If you let love and faith in Jesus dictates your actions then what you do and say will be in accordance with God's Word, because the Word is controlling you. If you let traditions of men; like evil acts and things contrary to God's Word dictate your actions, then what you do and say will be in accordance with things contrary to God's Word. Bottom line, you serve God by being loving, kind, caring, concern, understanding, forgiving, sharing, non-judgmental, a peace maker and

19

Joseph Haugabrook

positive to the people of the world. You must treat all
people as children of God. That is; you don't let physical
features and characteristics determine how you will respond
to them. Just remember what ever you do to your fellow man
you are doing it to God. And, when it comes to studying
God's Word, don't worry about not having a warm fuzzy or
strong urge to read the Bible; this will come with a steady
habit or daily reading. There are times you may have to
overcome things you've heard or seen; like hearing others
talk about how they are inspired to read the whole bible or
certain parts. Or you may hear: "If you don't get this urge or
inspiration you are doing something wrong and needs to get
closer to God." Well, I won't knock what others are doing or
saying, but no where in the bible have I found that a person
have to be inspired by God to read and understand his Word.
God doesn't force His Word on us, he makes it available and
gives an understanding of it but it's up to us to accept or
reject his Word. It all depends on whether we want to do right
or not. He urges us to learn of Him, which means to read and
ask for help when needed so we will understand what He
wants us to do in this life. God will provide an understanding
to any part of the bible we find difficult; either through
another person or a vision. But, God wants us to make up
our own mind to study His Word. There are times God will, if
we pray and ask for understanding of something happening
in our lives or something we want to overcome, send us a
specific scripture for the answer; as he did me at a time when
I was sincerely concerned about my children affairs; and he
sent me the 115th Psalm in a dream/vision. But these are the
specific things we are asking for and we have faith that he is
giving us what we are asking for. What I am saying is;
starting with the New Testament, read as least one chapter a

20

day. Don't skip about, and don't stop until you complete the entire New Testament. As you read, think only of yourself, and how close your words and deeds are to what the scriptures says they should be. There may be some scriptures; like the lineage of Jesus, that you don't understand why it's there, but don't try figuring it out if you don't know. Look at what it is saying and compare that to your life and the people you will interact with. For instant, the lineage of Jesus from Abraham to Joseph shows the different people; or races, we call them. This shows us that we, being his children, can't treat anyone or race as though they are not his child because his lineage contain all races; making us all his children and that's how he sees us. That is why it is so necessary to read the entire New Testament because from it we get our instructions on living under the New Covenant. Another example is the seven Churches in Revelation. Jesus is saying to us, and I'll put it in simple terms; you are among one of the seven spirits that is in the earth. Even though you may be different from a friend, and he differs from you, and, other people you both know; somewhere there is someone just like you; as with the others. The same goes for every other person. So in one of the seven churches, you will find yourself; which mean; you will find your strength or weakness. You will also know how God views you. And you will know what changes to make in your life. So when you read don't try and out guess the Word, just let it speak to you and accept what it's saying. If you are already doing what it says; rejoice and keep reading and using it to fine tune your life. If you are not doing what it says, adjust your life so it will be in compliance.

Again, don't be concerned about the desire or lack of

desire to read the bible. Whether you have a desire or not; make a habit for reading it daily. Read only to understand yourself. That is, to compare your thinking, responses, actions and reactions to people, places and things. Remember, you are the main focus here. God put you here, gave you instructions on how to live the life he gave you while you are here, so that you will be a part of his eternal plans both here on earth and afterward. And your bottom line instruction is; love the ones you see and interact with daily. The way you treat other people is the exact way you are treating God. And like it or not, those are our instructions. Remember, you live in the present, what you do this instant is the seed you plant. A minute ago is the past; a minute ahead is the future. When you look at someone and hate them at that instant you hate God. When you look at someone and love them, at that instant you love God. When you judge, at that instant you are telling God, I have to handle this case for you. You serve God by being loving and wanting the best for your fellow man. Read the bible to understand, first your self, then, how to treat others. Don't do it to try and understand God; but to obey, and trust God. When your life is aligned with the Word, you will have an understanding of God's love and His works. Just remember, understanding God's works begin with understanding yourself. After all, you are a part of God's work in action.

# The Reality Of God's Word

When using God's Word as a guide for your life, or teaching others, to use it to direct their lives, there are hard facts that have to be realized.

First it must be understood that whatever words God speaks becomes reality. God said "Let there be light." Light became reality. So did all other things in the heavens and earth. The Word later became flesh (to be a sacrificial lamb for our sins) and called Jesus; and performed what ever God said would be done. That has not changed. This fact is given to us in the Old and New Testaments. God told Abraham he would give him a son. Age was not a factor, God said it and it was done. God promised to hear the earnest prayer of his people. (We are all his people; some are good, some bad) Elijah asked that fire be sent from heaven to consume the altar; fire was sent. The Hebrew boys believed God would save them from the fiery furnace; they were saved. Peter and Paul asked in the name of Jesus and sick and lame people were healed. There is too much proof to even try and list it all here; you know that from reading the bible. The point I'm making is; when God speaks, his power make it happen. And nothing or no one but God can reverse it. So, when the Word of God says you are blessed; take it literally; because the blessing is a reality that no one but God can take away.

Some of the common questions of the, so called, modern age are: Why when I pray nothing happens? Why don't I see people being cured or raised from the dead by the laying on of hands, like it happened with the prophets, the disciples, and Jesus? Didn't Jesus say we would do even

Joseph Haugabrook

greater things than he did? Why does God let so many bad things happen? Why doesn't he stop all this evil people are committing? The questions are varied and many; and these are the things you are confronted with almost daily, whether you teach God's Word or not. The challenge here is to show that the Prophets, Disciples and Jesus lived by God's Word. And our lives must parallel the life of the Prophets, Disciples and Jesus in order to do what they did. You can't just live any ole way and expect God to perform what ever you ask of Him. You have to live according to His Word; like Jesus and the Prophets did. Jesus pointed it out many times in the New Testament; "Have faith in God; your faith have made you whole: Why did you fear." We can't be faithless and expect faith to work its perfect works in our lives. You, whether a teacher or not,  can be strong in your thinking, faith, and acceptance of reality, but you can only show and teach others, you can't change them; their acceptance of reality is the only thing that can do that. Remember the questions; "why does God let bad thing happen, or don't stop bad things from happening? Chances are, if God stopped every bad thing from happening, the person asking the question wouldn't be around to ask, what he's asking.

God set truth before us. He set reality before us, but he leaves it up to us to accept or reject it. He doesn't judge and mete punishment at the instant we contemplate or commit evil. Sure, every person will pay for their evil acts, but at a time and place set by God. This is one of the difficult things to accept and get others to see. Many are saying right now, they hate God because someone they loved died. They push aside the reality that everyone must die, even them. This is how thinking becomes selfish, and it's difficult to

24

break. However; truth, faith, and reality, will show many their selfish ways. It is important to know that no one can put across to others what they don't possess themselves. You can't give what you don't have. You can't teach what you don't know.

The New Testament is our guide for living in this world and obtaining eternal life. The promises made by Jesus are true and factual. They are reality and they are ours. The Old Testament is the examples of what happens when God speaks and men acts. It lists Gods promises to the people of that time, and the results of those promises. It shows what the people had to do in order to obtain the promises. It shows what happen when people rejected the promises, or passed God's Word off as superstition, a joke, or not being true.

Today, in present times, the New Testament is the reference to live by. Every word God spoke became reality. It exists, it's real, and it became reality when God spoke it. There is, however, something each individual has to do to obtain the promises listed in the New Testament. Because God gave us free will; that is; we can accept or refuse, God doesn't force his promises or blessing on us. He let us choose whether we want to receive them or not. If we choose to accept them; the things that must be done is outlined in the New Testament, and an example of it is given in the Old Testament. There is no doubt you have to know what to do in order to receive the promises. Every requirement, down to the letter, is given in the New Testament. That's why you have to read and read again the books in the New Testament. All instructions are found there. If you want to know results of any deed you do, good or bad, it can be found in the Old Testament. That is why we have no excuse of doing something and saying, "Well, I didn't know it would cause all this trouble, or pain." Every act committed by man today, the results can be found in the Old Testament. These are the facts that must be learned, lived, and taught. Love truth, and then teach it. Live faith, and then spread it. Accept reality, then, show it. Never pretend, because that is a lie, and God is never pleased with liars. And, if you are pretending in your teaching, it will come across as just that to your hearers. Whether you desire to just live the Word, teach it, or both; let truth and reality fill your acts and deeds. Love without exception; give, expecting nothing in return. Never rationalize or try to justify a wrong, no matter how small. Don't judge, belittle or adopt the holier than thou attitude. Look at the worst sinner with the same love, caring, concern, and understanding as you do the saint. Teach people how to be loving, caring, kind, understanding, be positive, have faith, and live each day as if they knew they were going to their maker tomorrow. Don't do it yourself, and don't try showing or teaching others outward actions; like shouting, speaking in tongues, and many such things. When they truly accept and practice the word of God in everything they do, their God given gift will manifest itself. And, it will be pleasing to God, because He gave it.

There are a lot of weeds in the field of life; don't try plucking them up; just feed them with the fertilizer God gave you and let God do the separating. You will never lose anything by helping; your barrel will stay full of meal and your pot full of oil. It's God's promise, and it is reality.

If you want to be a good doctor, lawyer, or any other

professional, you have to study, study, study, the necessary material. The same goes for being a good Christian. You must study, study, study, God's word.

## It's Important To Know God's Word

I say now, as always, to establishing a relationship with Jesus, it is important that you know the Word of God. I have and say again, read the bible often, preferably daily. Seek the answers to what it's saying about interacting with people, places and things. It's also important not to accept blindly, everything that's told to you, or you may read. I imagine if you don't know the meaning to a word you go to the dictionary and check it out. Use the same principle with the word of God. The bible is the acceptable source for understanding what God wants us to know about His program and our role in it. Your life is special to God, with a special purpose on this earth, and God did not put you here with a special thing to do and leave you without instructions on how to do it. What is happening to many; they get caught up in traditions and either forget or ignore the truth; that is, the Word of God. And notice, I didn't say books written explaining the Bible. The Bible is all you need to read, if you want the truth and facts about God, His creation, and where you fit in it all. It is perfectly fine to read how someone, through the Word of God, was blessed; financially, spiritually, physically or mentally. It can be very encouraging and comforting. Let's pose a question: Suppose you didn't know the difference between a wolf and a sheep but you knew the wolf was very dangerous to humans; while the sheep was not only safe but necessary for your survival. In the distance you see an animal approaching but you don't know whether it's a wolf or sheep. Someone standing with you tells you it is a sheep. They are only guessing because they want you to believe they are smart, and, right. Now, knowing that your very life could be destroyed if that person is wrong; wouldn't it make sense to leave and really learn the difference between a wolf and sheep and be safe, rather than take the chance of being destroyed? You will hear many things concerning the Word of God; but unless you know what's said is scriptural; then check it out using the bible. It's better to be safe than sorry. This is your life, your relationship with Jesus Christ; isn't it worth being safe? If you check the spoken words of man against the written Word of God, and the speaker has a problem with your action, don't worry about it; it's his or her problem, not yours. Your life and relationship depends on being right about the Word of God. Just remember; God didn't put His Word here to confound you, but rather to enlighten you about his perfect plan for you.

There are basics that must be adhered to in living for God

When I decided I wanted to drive, my first impression, from watching others, was; man this is easy! All I have to do is get behind the wheel, start the engine, put it in gear, steer it the way I wanna go, and stop when I get ready. Well, I did just that with a Model A Ford Coupe. I went forward and stopped it before hitting a barn in front of me. Then, I tried backing up. But when I tried stepping on the brakes I hit the gas instead and rammed into the smokehouse that was behind me. I hit it so hard it caved in a small section of the back corner of the smokehouse. My first reaction was panic. I had knocked a hole in the smokehouse where the canned fruits, vegetables, and smoke meats were kept. What was gonna happen to me when my folks found out? I was scared; not knowing what was coming. Well, if I had followed the basics of driving this wouldn't have happen. I should've learned about the pros and cons of driving before I got behind the wheel. My big mistake was just deciding one day I was going to drive and without any training, except watching others; I jumped behind the wheel. Living for God is no different; before you declare to others that you are living a Godly life, make sure you know what that entails. Don't just jump out there like I did behind the wheel, thinking you know because of what you've seen other do, but not knowing what the bible says. Get an understanding of God's Word from the bible, and make sure your life is in line with what the bible says before trying to demonstrate it to others. Many have been led astray because they followed what others were saying and doing without checking it against the Word of God; the bible.

It is a wonderful thing to teach God's Word. And let me hasten to add, the classroom is not always in some building with a captured audience. The teacher is your life, and the classroom is wherever you are at every instant of time. Knowing what God Word means and adapting it to your life is what teaching is all about. To believe and practice the love of God in your interaction with people is the way God wants us to teach his Word. Sure you will, at times, give the meaning to others; which mean you will teach it orally or through letters, to others. But, the greatest most effective way is to live it. You can't say you love a person and then be disrespectful, unkind, and uncaring at the same time. You can't abuse and care at the same time. You are your actions and reactions; that should always be at the forefront of your interactions.

The following four basics are very important but by no mean the only ones.

1. Believe that Jesus is the Son of God.

2. Read the four gospels; Matthews, Mark, Luke and John, and learn the examples Jesus set for us to live by.

3. Read the remaining New Testament to learn how Jesus, through his Disciples, set up his Church and how the Church is to operate.

4. Apply the teaching of Jesus to everything you do or say. That is, have faith in Jesus; believe He will honor every promise in the Bible.

As previously stated, these four are not the only important thing in living for God, but, they should be included in all interactions with people, places and things. These four will certainly put and keep you on the right road to serving God in the fullest. The only difficult part will be overcoming the doubts and fears that Satan will try to put in your heart. Having faith and trusting in Jesus Christ will prevent, or block, any attempt from Satan.

As stated in the topic; there are basics we have to observe if we want to be obedient to God's Word. It's like being a law abiding citizen. You obey the laws of the land; Nation, State, county and city. You don't run a red light because a policeman is not around. Nor park in a no-parking zone or drive the wrong way down a one way street. In short, you obey the laws because you know it will keep you out of trouble with the law.

Obeying the laws of God is no different. If you want to stay out of trouble with God; obey his laws. There is one big different between God and man's system. God sees us at all times. He knows every law we break and one day we'll have to give account of our actions. With man our worst crime can only result in death of the body; that is, put to death by man's system. With God we are not only put to death, our souls can end up in hell. So obeying God's law becomes very important.

There is another important point to add: going to church. Many believe that just going to church satisfy their requirement to God. It is commonly believed that one hour on Sunday morning; singing hymns selected by the pastor or musician; listening to prayers and a sermon which, by the way, must be completed in one hour, is all that is required to serve God. The rest of the week, except maybe Wednesday night bible class, is spent doing their own thing. Simply put; going to church can be compared to a person going to the filling station each week to fill up his car with gas. You have a full tank of gas; now what do you do with it? Do you just drive back to your house and let the car set idling, burning gas until next weekend? Is every tank full of gas you get, used up with your car idling in the driveway? On your way home from the station do you use your car to run down people, or try to harm them in some way? If you drive pass a person mired in a ditch, carrying a heavy load, do you stop to give a helping hand? What are you doing with the gas you get each weekend? We go to church to learn how to interact with people according to the Word of God. We learn how to live our lives according to his word. We learn what love, compassion, caring, understanding and cooperation are. We learn how to use love to make our homes and communities a better place to live. In short; we learn how to apply God's Word in everything we do and say. We go to church and get our tank filled so we can take the goodness of God to others. Leaving church and going home to do nothing except wait for next Sunday is not the reason for attending church. Seeing others in need and not trying to help in some way is using the gas you got from church to drive pass others without giving a helping hand. Take what you have been given freely and help others.

This is not to criticize anyone for attending church. Nor to say you shouldn't attend church. Yes, by all means, attend church. I do say you don't rush services. I do say attend with the idea of getting something to help self and others, keeping both on the same level. You will find that your efforts will help a lot of people to live better lives if you do.

Whether you read the Word of God to further your own understanding, or teach it to someone else; concentrating on the following topics and applying them will keep you in the right frame of mind when interacting with people, places and things.

Life is not according to man. The universe and the laws governing it are fixed. The sun and other heavenly bodies, including earth, will always react according to the laws of the universe. The effects of the moon on the waters will always be according to the laws of the universe. God made and fixed everything. God allows us to imitate, even duplicate, but we can't change what he has fixed in place. His Word tells us how to live a happy successful life. It's all fixed. If we live according to his Word, we can have just what the Bible promise us. We break God's laws and then blame him for the punishment he tells us before hand will come upon us. Do you blame the policeman for giving you a ticket when you run a red light? Do you blame the instructor giving you a bad grade when you fail to follow the instruction on the test? Do you blame the employer for firing you if you fail to perform according to the job requirements?

Follow the instruction given by God. Read the bible, learn the commandments and do accordingly.

Things that are a must in being obedient to Jesus Christ.

## BELIEVE

Mark 16:16  He that believeth and is baptized shall be saved; but he that believeth not shall be damned.
John 3:15-16
: 15  That whosoever believeth in him should not perish, but have eternal life.

33

:16  For God so loved the world, that he gave his only begotten Son, that whosoever believeth in him should not perish, but have everlasting life

John 11:26  And whosoever liveth and believeth in me shall never die. Believeth thou this?

Roman 10:10    For with the heart man believeth unto righteousness; and with the mouth confession is made unto salvation.

Look at belief from a personal viewpoint. There are many benefits in believing Jesus is the son of God. Believing is the first step in establishing a relationship with Jesus. Believing that He is and His Word is truth give a firm foundation on which to form every action and reaction in daily interaction with nouns.

There are peace and harmony in believing. Think about your children, spouse or close friend. Trusting them; believing you can rely on their word no matter what; is very reassuring, especially in times of need. Times when you need someone to talk to about things you don't want to share with anyone else; or when you need a favor of some kind. Having someone to turn to for help, is a very good feeling. Especially knowing it's always there, whether needed or not. Believing in Jesus; provides these and many more benefits. No one has ever regretted believing in Jesus.


## FAITH


Matthews 6:25 Therefore I say take no thought for your life, what ye shall eat, or what ye shall drink; not yet for your body, what ye shall put on. Is not the life more that meat, and the body than raiment?

34

# Let's Talk About Jesus

Mark 11:22 And Jesus answering saith unto them, Have faith in God.
Luke 7:50  And he said to the woman, Thy faith hath saved thee; go in peace.

Faith is the mighty force that guides the lives of believers. It is the tool given by God to gain access to all the things promised in his Holy Word. It is the power to squash doubting, especially when asking Jesus for something. Faith is that perfect assurance that we are going to get whatever we ask in the name of Jesus.

One of my daughters said to me one day. You know daddy, when we were kids we never worried about anything. When we asked for something, whether foods, clothing, or toys, we knew we could expect them. Asking and getting never crossed our minds, even if we didn't get it right away. Now that she has her own children she does the same for them.
Faith is a very powerful tool. It is a yard stick for the things we receive from Jesus. If someone gives you a one mile tape measure and tell you the land you measure off will be the land you own; and you only measure off a few inches, you can't blame anyone but yourself for what you end up with. God has given us unlimited faith. We can use it to obtain the many blessings he has in his storehouse. If we choose to limit ourselves then we can only blame ourselves. Remember Jesus told us; "According to your faith be it unto you." Faith is our yardstick; we have to use it.

## PRAYER

Matthews 7:7-11 Ask and it shall be given you; seek, and ye shall find; knock, and it shall be opened unto you;

:8 For everyone that asketh receiveth; and he that seeketh findeth; and to him that knocketh it shall be opened.

:9 Or what man is there of you, whom if his son ask bread, will he give him a stone:

:10  Or if he ask a fish will he give him a serpent?

:11  If ye then, being evil, know how to give good gifts unto your children, how much more shall your Father which is in heaven give good things to them that ask him.
Matthews 6:6-13
:6 But thou, when thou prayest, enter into thy closet, and when thou hast shut thy door, pray to thy Father which is in secret; and thy Father which seeth in secret shall reward thee openly.

:7 But when ye pray, use not vain repetitions, as the heathen do; for they think that they shall be heard for their much speaking.

:8 Be not ye therefore like unto them; for your Father knoweth what things ye have need of, before you ask him.

:9 After this manner therefore pray ye: Our Father which are in heaven, Hallowed be thy name,

:10 Thy kingdom come. Thy will be done in earth, as it is in heaven

:11 Give us this day our daily bread.

:12 And forgive us our debts, as we forgive our debtors.

:13 And lead us not into temptation but deliver us from evil: For thine is the kingdom, and the power, and the glory, for ever. Amen.

Prayer is giving undivided attention to Jesus while talking to Him. There are many reason for talking with Jesus; thankfulness, asking a special blessing for self or others; needing guidance; to name a few. God is a Spirit, Jesus is a spirit. So, talking to Him must be done in spirit and truth.

Jesus sees the hearts and knows, even before asked, what is needed, why it's needed, why we are asking; and how we intend to use it. And remember, Jesus is not a part nor will become a part of little games; like granting prayers so we can brag, or surpass the Jones; look big or important; or, some other vain reason. Jesus is not about sending souls to hell; but rather sharing his glory. He is about things that matters; like, enjoying the beauty He put on earth, and what He has prepared in Heaven for believers. But, talking to Him must be done in truth. No one can fool Jesus; so let your prayers be truthful and honest, and the needs asked for legitimate; even a desire to be better overall. He will give it to you but not break his own rules to do it.

Joseph Haugabrook

## FORGIVENESS

Luke 6:37 Judge not, ands ye shall not be judged; condemn not, and ye shall not be condemned; Forgive and ye shall be forgiven:

Man has coined all kind of phrases regarding forgiveness which will not be mentioned because whether I agree or disagree is not important. The important thing is your action and reaction toward people, places and things, and the attitude while responding.

Someone trespass against you; what's the correct response: forgive or seek revenge? You trespass against someone; what's the correct response: ask forgiveness or try justifying your action?

Failing to forgive, are not acting within the laws of God. If forgiveness is desired; it must also be given. God forgive our trespasses when we forgive the trespasses of others. Plain and simple; God will forgive us if we forgive others.

There is beauty and peace in forgiving; giving a joy that spreads through the body and soul. On the other hand, a heavy load is associated with revenge. It causes stress, frustration, tiredness, even illnesses, not to mention the attitudes associated with stress, and frustration. Never believe revenge is sweet. Even if one feels some kind of elation, it's short lived; because the reality of your actions will set in and when it does, it brings with it; untold misery. Remember this: revenge is bitterness; Forgiveness is sweet.

Let's Talk About Jesus

## TRUTH SHALL SET YOU FREE

Matthews 11:21 Woe unto thee, Chorazin! Woe unto thee, Bethsaida! For if the mighty works, which were done in you, had been done in Tyre and Sidon, they would have repented long ago in sackcloth and ashes.

Luke 13:28 There shall be weeping and gnashing of teeth, when ye shall see Abraham and Isaac, and Jacob, and all the prophets in the kingdom of God, and you yourselves thrust out.

You shall know the truth and the truth shall make you free.

Whether you look at it from a spiritual, physical, scientific, or just a plain ole common sense, those words are totally true and a hundred percent effective. Cures for diseases, illnesses, problems, of all kinds have been found by first learning the truth about them. Learning how something works what it thrives on and its effect; are the first steps in getting rid of it.

You have a problem you want to get rid of, the first question is: what can I do? Example: a legitimate case of spousal abuse: husband beats the wife. What's the solution to this horrible problem? The problem is with the person; the husband. He has the problem and must understand that he does. He has to know the reason why he hits his wife. He has to learn the real truth about himself. The spotlight has to be focused on him and him alone. He allows himself to get angry: why? He allows himself to raise his hands and strike: why? He allows himself to commit the horrible acts: why? The person committing the acts; good or bad; is the one that has, within, the ability to abstain, and is therefore responsible. It all goes back to knowing the truth and walking in light. If we walk in darkness there is a good chance for stumbling; and as long as the person with the problem refuse to admit there is a problem, that person is walking in darkness.

Jesus told us that he is the light of the world. That is, if we let our actions and reactions be in accordance with his teachings we will understand how to interact with people, places and things.

It is ironic that with all the advance technology, instant communication world wide, instant availability of information on every subject imaginable, we are still in the dark on the plaguing problems of society. Families are being torn apart by unruly disrespectful, ungrateful children, unfaithful, abusive spouses, and the list goes on. The nation is being divided by lying, deceitful politician. The church is losing its effectiveness by watering down the word of God and seeking money more than souls; and the people in general are losing faith in everything but self, because that is the only thing they have that they can trust; Why? Because men are groping around in complete darkness trying to find their way; they are trying to make lies work as truth.

If you want to rid yourself and community of selfish politics, greed in religious, social and racial inequality, fiction in history and social sciences, and, all named problems; do what Jesus said: learn truth, act on it; reject man developed terms and phrases designed to make one group of people appear superior to another; thus pitting them against each other. Love truth; make it a part of every interaction with nouns.

Let's Talk About Jesus

What's Happening In The Church?

Jesus Actions Toward Corruption In The Church:

Matthew 21:12-13

:12 And Jesus went into the temple of God, and cast out all them that sold and bought in the temple, and overthrew the tables of the moneychangers, and the seats of them that sold doves,

:13 And said unto them, It is written My house shall be called the house of prayer; but ye have made it a den of thieves.

These two scriptures alone are enough to make everyone examine themselves and, look at what's going on in their temple. Never mind the structure, or building, attended each week to fellowship and hear the word of God; look at self and what's being done in the congregation; especially the leaders: pastor, deacon, and those in leadership roles. What is being done? What is allowed? Ask yourself; what have you become? What are you accepting into your life? What are you siding with? What truth and facts are you ignoring to be called a modernist? What are you doing for personal gain, and is it violating the word of God? And, is the congregation you are associated with allowing thing that violate the word of God?

Jesus went into the temple and ran out those that were doing things for personal gain: greed in other words. The same thing is happening to many today. All kinds of efforts and deeds are taking place in church buildings and in the heart because it has been determined to be what's right in modern times. But, when such thinking is allowed to take shape, it says plainly that the Word of God is old fashioned and out of touch with modern times, and, reality. Which says God didn't know what his creation would evolve into and therefore His teaching, as written, can't be used, in modern times, This is not only wrong it's dangerous to human stability. To find the unknown, there must be a known. For a man to find the solution to his problems he first must know that a known exist. Not knowing is the reason for man struggling and not finding solutions to his problem. He is not using the known; Jesus Christ; to affect solutions to the problems he faces.

Look at what Jesus did in the temple. He said His house is a house of prayer. He compared the actions of those in the temple to the Word of God. It was not even close, so he drove them out. Our actions and deeds are causing the problems in the world today. We are trying to start with the unknown to find a solution. Hitch the horse to the wagon properly and there won't be a problem getting it rolling. Righteousness will not be gained through greed, selfishness, and like things that causes problems. Jesus drove out the elements that produce problem and confusions. He will do the same for us today if we invite Him into our lives. Anything that is not according to His word will be driven out, leaving us clean and our deeds acceptable. Examine yourself today and see if anything that shouldn't be has slipped in.

# Let's Talk About Jesus

## A Time Of Reflection

### Truth, Facts, Reality

It's difficult sometimes to watch people being bound and shackled by the many facets of society. Fear has become a giant monster driving people behind well secured doors. Addictions are wreaking havoc in families and communities. Children are becoming unruly, causing family, community and nations, untold headaches. Churches are becoming more concerned about being politically correct than spiritually correct. Community, state and national leaders try harder to find an excuse, or cover-up, for a misgiving than a factual, lasting solution. People in general have drifted into a state of instance; everything must be now; immediate; if not, I'll try something else. If a marriage is in trouble the couple look for a quick fix. If the children are developing bad habits; again, look for a quick fix. A quick fix has become the trend of the day. And, it is causing damage of epic proportion in thinking, attitudes, practices and beliefs. If you believe what you see on small and large screens you would believe that God created reproduction (now being paraded as sex) for fun and games. The practice of using the body as a test, to see whether a man and woman can live together in harmony and peace (now called compatibility) has reached a shameful level. If that's the reason for marriage then, the marriage is doomed from the start. Reproduction should be like mittens used to lift hot items; only used for the purpose intended. Reproduction is meant to bring children into the world; it's not music you dance to, or a sport you play. It should be used when a couple get married and decide it's time to start a family.

Joseph Haugabrook

But, let's not stray too far a field; let's stay focused on truth. We see all the things men are becoming mired in. We see all the ways that are being tried to get out of the mire. We hear ranting and raving about this, and that, solution. We watch and listen to all these things, and yet, the same mire is holding men fast. Is there a solution to the plaguing problems of man? Of course it is; but it will not be found except in truth. Jesus didn't tell us man would devise a way to get out of troubles. He didn't say look to those who we esteem as political leaders, professional counselors and such, for solutions. Jesus never said man ways would set us free from the problems facing man. He said truth would set us free.

Think about this one problem and look at how it can be solved. Racial tension is a giant problem in America. The fuel feeding this tension is misunderstanding, or, a lack of truth. If American Caucasians and American Blacks would put truth in all of their interactions, starting with the subjects educating our children, tension would evaporate like a drop of water on a Georgia cement road in mid August. Truth, fact, reality, it's what going to straighten out the mess men have made for themselves.

# Let's Talk About Jesus

## God Didn't Create The Mess Mankind Is Experiencing

Genesis 1:31

:31 And God saw everything that He had made and behold it was very good. And the evening and the morning were the sixth day.

On the sixth day of creation, God looked at everything he had made and saw that it was very good. So there is no question that God created a system of good; because God himself declared it. Note one thing about the creation, no where in all the things God created can any of the mess we are now experiencing be found. I don't have to itemize the evils we wade through each day, you know them as well as I do. So the question becomes, since God made it good; why the mess now? Better yet, since God didn't make it a part of his creation; why are men trying to insert it into God's programs now? And why would man think he can make something God didn't create as part of his process. God didn't create, lies, hatred, envy, adultery, greed of all kinds; lust, addictions, abuse of all kinds, and all the evils that man are donning and shaping to fit him like the clothing he wears. Evil was not a part of God's programs in the beginning and it still isn't. Good and evil, or right and wrong will never mix. So, as you make preparation for each day's journey, remember, to put in their proper place, the parts God created and the part he left out. Want a happy life? Use the parts God created to build it.

Joseph Haugabrook

God's Commandment To All Living Things To Fill The Earth With Its Kind.

Genesis 1:20 - 28

:20 Then God said, Let the waters bring forth abundantly the moving creatures that hath life and fowl that may fly above the earth in the open firmament of heaven.

:21 And God created great whales, and every living creature that moveth, which the waters brought forth abundantly, after their kind and every winged fowl after his kind: and God saw that it was good.

:22 And God Blessed them, saying, "Be fruitful and multiply, and fill the waters and the sea, and let fowls multiply on the earth."

:23 So the evening and the morning were the fifth day.

:24 Then God said "Let the earth bring forth the living creature according to its kind; cattle and creeping thing and beast of the earth, after his kind: and it was so.

:25 And God made the beast of the earth after his kind, cattle after their kind and every thing that creepeth upon the earth after his kind: and God saw that it was good.

:26 And God said, "Let us make man in our image, after our likeness: and let them have dominion over the fish of the sea, And over the fowl of the air, and over the cattle, And over all the earth, And over every creeping thing that creepeth upon

46

the earth.

:27 So God created man in His own image; in the image of God created He him; male and female created He them.

:28 And God blessed them, and God said to them. "Be fruitful and multiply; and replenish the earth, and subdue it: and have dominion over the fish of the sea, And over the fowl of the air and over every living thing that moveth upon the earth.

Right out of the gate; man should get this right, because God gave mankind the responsibility of being caretakers of the earth and its abundance. Mankind is to take what God created and shape, and reshape it into things for the betterment of life. To build up, not destroy. Enhance not make worse. Pay close attention to the phrase; "after its kind." God created the living things of the sea; the winged things that fills the heavens (skies) the creeping things that fill the earth (from tiny creeping things to the largest animal). God specifically said to each different creature; "Bring forth others after your kind." In other words when God said "Be fruitful and multiply" He was saying to each specific kind of animal, fish and bird, use the means I have given you to bring others like you into the world. Fill it up with your kind. Note: God specifically identified different creatures of the sea, land and air as "kinds." (Modern science have grouped and named them species). Therefore, these creatures can be seen and expected to mate or reproduce with their own kind. They can even be expected to interact only with their kind. So, there is nothing wrong if cattle separate themselves from moose or some other wild animal of the forest. It is quite normal for a praying mantis to separate itself from the grasshopper; especially when it comes to reproducing its own kind. Look at kinds: Robins, blue birds, sparrows, crows etc; kinds of birds; Salmons, whales, sharks, red snapper, mullets, etc; kinds of fish. Kinds of animals are; Elk, Deer, Antelope, Bison, Cattle, etc. Now, look at verse 26-28. "Let us make man in our image, according to our likeness." God said to them, "Be fruitful and multiply." Did God say let us make different kinds of men? Did God say let us make men in our image? (In the beginning was the Word, and the Word was with God and the Word was God. The Word became flesh, and named Jesus; so, God and Jesus are one There is no Caucasian God, African God, Chinese God, Mexican God; etc, and etc. One God; and man is made in the image and likeness of God.

God formed man from the dust of the earth, and from man, God made Woman, and blessed them and gave them the same commandment he gave to everything in the sea, air and on land; reproduce your own kind. The fact that some, because of climatic conditions and sometimes health problems, have developed different skin colors does not change the truth of man's creation. Identifying people according to color and developed habits (customs) was done by man and man alone. Separating people into groups and separating groups according to man developed preferences can only be contributed to man. God created man to interact and reproduce according to God's commandment. There is no different kind of man. Accepted or not, man was created in the image and likeness of God; and the love between men should be the same as between God and Jesus.

Just for a moment think about verse 26 and 27. I

mean really and deeply consider what those two verses are saying. God made man and woman in His image. We are the exact reflection of God. That is why it is no great mystery that we, just like Jesus, can love, be very good, kind and compassionate to people we interact with daily. We can be holy; and all the righteous things God's Word says we can be. You probably have one picture some place that you are very proud of. When you look at that picture you see an exact reflection of you when it was taken; nice smile; clothing in place, pose just right. God created us to be like him; and loved us so much that he made us to rule over what he had placed on earth. Just like your picture, when God looks at us he should see a reflection of himself; the very thing he created; everything perfect just like He created it. Wouldn't you be upset if the picture you loved was vandalized by someone mad at you just because you wouldn't listen to his lies that would mess up your whole family? You wouldn't be upset at the picture, but you would be at the act of vandalism.

You are the image of God; loving, caring, understanding, powerful, and all the positives recorded in the bible. Look at the word "powerful." You have within you the ability to accomplish every thing Jesus told us we could accomplish. Moses secured the release of a nation without making one promise of benefit to the captor. An army bent on destroying him was itself destroyed without an arrow being shot or sword raised. The power of God flows through you, His image, to accomplish great things with the tool God gives you; but not through a distorted reflection representing His image. Restore God's image to its originality and you will be successful in all your endeavors.

Again; think about who you really are. You are the very image of God! Think about God and what He is. Then know that you are just like Him. I once found an old table. On the surface it didn't look like very much, but I liked its shape and the way it was made. I didn't know until I removed several coats of cracking ugly, faded paint, that I had a rare antique item. You may have something covering the real you; the beautiful reflection of God. And, if you are not reflecting the very thing you know God is, then remove whatever is distorting the real image of what you should be.

Again; think, concentrate, meditate, and look at all the inner strength you possess. You are a powerful individual. Through the Blood of Jesus, God sees the very thing he created, making you eligible to receive every promised blessing. Don't be afraid or ashamed to be every good thing the bible says you can be; because in reality; you are; think about it!

Reality: Every human being on the face of the earth came from the one man God created. That make mankind one. Just because we separate ourselves by color, religion, size, eyes and the likes, does not make it truthful or reality. These are man developed preferences to establish him as smarter, stronger, prettier, and other vain desires; and must be seen for what they truly are. These are mountain climbers trying to reach the stars by climbing clouds. God specified what he wanted his creations to be known as...Kinds; and that especially includes man.

A misunderstanding of the creation of man exist because accepting the truth would erase man developed preferences to raise individuals, or group, above another; and thus, in the mind of man, diminish his status.

## Let's Talk About Jesus

## The Great Gift From God

1 John 3:1-3

:1 Behold, what manner of love the Father hath bestowed upon us, that we should be called the sons of God; therefore the world knoweth us not, because it knew him not.

:2 Beloved, now are we the sons of God, and it doth not yet appear what we shall be; but we know that, when he shall appear, we shall be like him; for we shall see him as he is.

:3 And every man that hath this hope in him purifieth himself, even as he is pure.

Look at the great gift of love the Father has given his children. No one knowing the Word of God can doubt that to be called the children of God is a great honor.

Thinking about what that means is mind boggling. To be called the children of God, by God, means we are doing what pleases him. And that means all the good that God has provided are readily available to us. I would never try outlining all the good things God have available to us; for it would take more books than all the libraries on earth could hold.

However, we know that accepting this great gift, that is, letting love guide our thoughts, efforts, actions and reactions, we become that individual that God created in his own image; with the key to all the goods that he provided for his children to enjoy on this earth.

One thing that we should always keep in mind; God meant for this life on earth to be enjoyable; but it can only happen if we believe in the Word, and have faith to trust Him fully. I know it's difficult to see peace, serenity, love and understanding with so much confusion, hate, violence and wars raging all around us. But this is where our faith goes to work. There is no need for a soldier to put his survival training into action until he is faced with a situation that requires it. He fires his weapon at the enemy because the situation requires it. He uses every means at his disposal to defeat the enemy and preserve his life because the situation requires it. Think how ineffective a soldier would be if he had to face a well trained well armed enemy without any training on what to do, or how to handle himself, or the weapons available to him. He would likely be defeated in short order. All of God's children are faced with the present of the enemy (Satan) each day; and enemy that is trying to destroy, not just the body, but also the soul; an enemy that wants to deceive, disgraces, and finally, destroy us. And make no mistake, he will, unless we know what weapons are available to us; learn to use them, and apply them each time the situation requires it.

We, as children of God, have the weapons to fight the enemy (Satan) that's constantly trying to destroy us. And, since he is always in our face, we should always know what weapon to fire to get him out of our way. This is not to say we should call each individual that frown at us or say something nasty, or look the other way to keep from looking at us; a devil. But we should recognize that this is not an act of a God fearing individual; ignore it, and not let it determine our action toward them. Our action should be determined by our training from God's word. We know from the Word of God we don't hate because someone hate us. We don't cuss because we are cussed at. We don't do sinful things because sin is all around us. We know what our training dictates; and to preserve our life and soul we will follow our training when faced with acts of the enemy. Sure the enemy will say things in an attempt to inflame, confuse or cause us to change our minds and ways; that is his job; he's trying to get us to come to his side. That is; doing things his way; hating, cussing, warring, lying, cheating, and committing horrendous acts of sin. Don't expect anything less from him. He hates us and wants us to destroy ourselves by doing his bidding. But, regardless of what comes, we have the assurance of God, who controls the universe, that we can be in his family; enjoying his present which brings love, peace, understanding, cooperation, and all the positive things of life on this earth when we use his Words to guide our actions and reactions toward people we encounter each day.

The good life can be had right here on earth by all God's children; but we must use the training that comes only from his Word to obtain it. Those who don't have the same training won't understand the actions of God's children, and will surely say negative things about them. But it's not A Christian's job to take these negative things to heart. Their job is to obey the Word. Don't worry about how it appear to others; just know that as long as we are living like God tells us to live we are, as He said; his image. And when we one day see Him we will know that we are like him. If we live in the Word and the Word live in us we are the image of God; this, my friends, to use a commonly used phrase; is the good life.

Joseph Haugabrook

## It Is A Gift From God

Ephesians 2:1, 8-9

:1 And you hath he quickened, who were dead in trespasses and sin.

:8 For by grace you are saved through faith, and not of yourselves; it is the gift of God,

:9 Not of works, lest anyone should boast.

A brief summation of chapter two is this: Jesus loved us to the point of becoming flesh and taking upon himself the sins of us all and suffered the punishment for those sins, just to save us from our own deeds. There is no comparison to this kind of love and sacrifice; but, using mankind's language I compare it to a man that had and enjoyed the very best that life could offer. No matter what you can think of, or imagine, this man had the best. One day he walks into a prison full of rapists, murders, robbers, adulterers, liars and worse and willingly accept whatever punishment these prisoners had coming, and let them all go free to enjoy the best life had to offer; the same thing he had enjoyed. The prisoners didn't have to do or promise the man anything for his sacrifice; he just set them free out of love for them. And, the only thing the prisoners had to do to stay out of jail and keep enjoying the glorious things of life were to follow the same rules and regulations the man was following. Think about that! Let's say you are in jail, faced, along with other prisoners, the just punishment for your crimes; you nor the prisoners with you have any hope of enjoying the good of society. But, in walk a man, opens the doors of the prison, and instantly you are free. Nothing was required on your part to receive this great gift. You gave nothing, you offered nothing, and you promised nothing. You just walked out of prison a free person. In fact some of you that was being freed by the man ridiculed him, some wanted to kill him, some even involved themselves in the act of having him put in a position so they could kill him. Yet, in spite of these negative destructive actions, the man still set everyone free. The only thing the man said was; in your interaction with people places and things, treat them as I've treated you. The man knew if your action were in accordance with his instructions you would be following the same rules and guidelines that he followed; thus guaranteeing you all the wonderful things of life, both in this world and the world to come. The man loved you and wanted you to enjoy the good things of life and the only way that could happen was for your record to be cleared; so he accepted your punishment so your slate would be clean.

In your bible class, group study, family gathering, or wherever you discuss the Word of God, keep in mind, Jesus gave you the gift of a wonderful life in this world and the world to come. No one can brag about his or her position in God's program. Wherever you are, it's not because of any work you've done, it because Jesus loved you and forgave your sins. The same benefits you are enjoying are available to every other human being on earth. The only requirement for any human being to enjoy the glorious life of God is follow the teachings of Jesus. Because, if you follow the teaching of Jesus, you will love others as he loves you. Therefore, you will not lie, commit adultery, murder, steal, bear false witness, cheat, commit acts of selfish gain, pretend, or commit any act that is contrary to the teaching of Jesus.

If you think you are better, holier; and greater than anyone else, you better look at your deeds and ask yourself, who made me judge! And don't give me this, "I can tell an apple from an orange." You may well tell the difference, but that is only recognition. You may recognize that the orange or apple is bad, or good, for your health, but you certainly didn't receive a commandment from God to judge it, something He made and put on this earth. If the orange has a rotten spot on it, whose fault is it; the orange; or the tender of the orange? The thing to do is learn the difference between recognizing something and judging it. God judges; man is only to recognize, accept or reject. Accepting and rejecting means you say to yourself; this is not what God Word says to do. Or, this is what God Word says to do. To put it another way; if a person is allowing a sinful act to manifest itself in him or her, they don't condemn the person or the act, just recognize that it is something they will not allow to happen in their life and walk away from it with their mouth closed and their mind reacting in love. Just remember the rot on the orange or the blight on the apple is there because the tenders of the crops fell down on their responsibilities. If the orchard keepers don't know what spray to use to prevent rot and blight, they should consult the experts. God said He would heal the land if: those who are called by My name would humble themselves and pray and seek My face." In other words; if the people calling themselves God children would live according to the Word of God, God would heal our land today. Look at Sodom when

Abraham interceded for the city, God told Abraham he would not destroy it if Abraham could fine ten righteous men in it. Oops, Abraham couldn't find ten; plenty of people in that great city, but where were their righteous deeds. Sound like any of our big cities today?

Bragging and boasting creates vain egos; and egos make a person set him or herself above others in their minds. And that, ladies and gentlemen, is contrary to the teaching of Jesus. In simple words, you are sinning against God. God Word is reality, anything else is a lie; created and perpetuated by Satan. If you've ever sinned, in anyway, you can't judge sin in any form. Only God who has never sinned can judge sin.

## Be Fruitful And Multiply

Genesis 2:20 - 24

:20 And Adam gave names to all cattle, to the fowls of the air, and to every beast of the field. But for Adam there was not found an help meet for him.

:21 And the Lord God caused a deep sleep to fall upon Adam, and he slept; and He took one of his ribs and closed up the flesh instead thereof.

:22 And the rib, which the Lord God had taken from man, made he a woman, and brought her unto the man.

:23 And Adam said: this is now bone of my bones and flesh of my flesh; she shall be called woman, because she was taken out of man.

:24 Therefore shall a man leave his father and mother and shall cleave unto his wife: and they shall be one flesh.

To start; focus on verse 24. "But for Adam there was not found an help meet for him."

First; ask yourself; what was it that Adam needed help doing? Was it to name the birds of the air or the beast of the field? Was it to tend the garden or select which foods to eat? Note: Adam was able to do everything God commanded of him except one: "Be fruitful and multiple." That is, bring forth your own kind. Every living thing on earth was given the commandment to reproduce others like itself; including Adam. Was God unaware of the fact that he had created only a male which, as it stood, was incapable of completely fulfilling his commandment? God forbid! God knew exactly what he was doing. And, it is one of the great lessons you will find in the bible, in patience, and obedience in fulfilling God's commandments.

As Adam went about his work; naming the swimming, flying and creeping things of the earth, he was well aware that each thing named had a mate to bring others like it into the world. The desire to bring others like him into the world dwelled in Adam because it was a commandment from God. But, it was not an urge to engage in the reproductive act just for fun, or the excitement of it. Adam, like other living things, needed a female or helper to fully comply with God's commandment. So, God, in his own time, took a part of the male (rib) and made female. Adam knew from whence Eve came and called that part of him "woman" meaning, a part of me has been made female. Adam now had the one thing he needed to completely comply with God's commandments. Now, from this point on when the desire, or urge, to reproduce manifested itself in Adam and Eve, they obeyed accordingly; which brought forth their children. Adam did many other wonderful things in this God given example, but let's just concentrates on patience and reproduction.

Patience: To understand Adam's patience, first understand that created in every human being is the desire to obey the Word of God, or to conduct your life according to truth and holiness. God's work is truth and holiness; you are the image of God; God didn't create in you something that was not of him, nor did he leave anything out. You have the power to do things exactly as God has commanded. If you believe whole heartedly, without wavering in the slightest, you can accomplish what God said you can.

Adam, as he worked, had this constant yearning to do all that God had told him to do. And even though he didn't have all he needed to completely comply he didn't grumbling or complaining. Adam knew God. Knowing God gives us the mind and attitude to do every righteous thing we can without questioning God about what's lacking. And, not trying to do something we think will fulfill God's will without God providing the means. Adam knew, without a shadow of doubt that he was to be a part of bringing others, like himself into the world, yet there was no means to do it, until God provided it, so he patiently waited. Ladies and gentlemen,

God knows what He is doing, so exercise patience and wait; rushing only serve to get you in deep trouble.

Adam didn't attempt to try anything but God's way in the reproductive process. Again, he worked and waited. We know the flying and creeping things by name, because Adam was obedience in using the means God provided. Was there more to Adam's actions? Yes, much more, but it will not be covered here. We want to stay focused on the important topic of humans bringing forth other humans. Adam was patience while waiting for the means to carry out God's commandment to reproduce. So I can say to you; don't rush it; be patience and obedient and look to God for that mate. Sure Satan will make you think you have to do certain things men and women desire of you in order to find a mate. But I say; hog wash! Just learn God's way and follow it.

Reproduction: When the time was right (by God's will, not Adam) God put into motion the means for Adam to fulfill the commandment to be fruitful and multiply. From Adam, God took a rib and created Eve. Now the unit for reproduction was complete. Which brings us to the yearning, longing or desire, men so often speak of as existing in Adam. That yearning was not urges to engage in the reproductive act, it was a desire to obey Gods commandment to fill the earth with humans. In providing the means to do this God did something very unique for mankind. God didn't go back to the dust of the earth to create flesh, he took the flesh he had already created and made female; now two individuals existed from one flesh; which brings in the saying (reality); the two are one. The other unique thing God did was to make the process produce exactly what he had created. God also set in motion a process that would keep things equal between all males and females of their kinds. Every woman has the same reproductive units. Every male have the same reproductive units. No woman have two or three sets of reproductive units, and no male have two or three sets of reproductive units. Bottom line, the vital parts of the reproductive process is the same in all women and all men. God made all females the same and all males the same. No man or woman can boast of being different, where it really matters. Keep in mind, things like facial features, skin color, body sizes and shape, color and length of hair, large hands, large feet, etc. and etc., are physical attributers having nothing to do with the reproductive process, and are personal preferences driven by individual desires. One individual like another based on something of a personal choices/reasons, but, the bottom line is; all these things are vain desires derived from teachings, beliefs, and practices.

Today, "sex" has overshadowed reproduction. Sex has become one of the greatest money makers of our times. It's in newspapers, on radios, splashed across television and movie screens, on the internet; in fact it is the dominant factor of sales from tooth picks to moon rockets. It has become the number one factor for male/female dating. It is being portrayed as joy, pleasure, and all the descriptive words/terms formed for lust. God did not create a process studded with lustful desires and acts. Look at the way God set the process in action. The urge or desire to engage in the act of reproduction came when God created Eve and brought her to Adam blessed them and told them to bring forth other little Adams and Eves. God's process does not provide for male on male or female on female to complete the act. It has to be as God created it. Note again, "For this cause." This cause is referring to the process of reproduction. Today, this cause is called marriage. But also note, Eve is Adam's flesh, and man must know, female is him and as he treats female, so is he treating himself. Female must know, she is man's flesh and as she treats the male so is she treating herself. And regardless of what is taught or believed, the truth stands; God have not changed the process he created. Every woman is some man's rib.

To be in compliant with God's commandment every man and woman must, as Adam did, wait until his/her mate is given and blessed by God before engaging in the reproductive act. In other words, be as patience and obedient as Adam. Interact with males and females as God's Word provides. God didn't bring Eve to Adam and say; "here try her out and see if the two of you are compatible." He didn't say; here, take this female and have yourself some fun." And he certainly didn't say, "Take this female and use her for personal profit. The male and female reproductive units are sacred items to be used only in the process of bringing another human being into the world. Remember everything God made is good. He provided beauty and joy in everything he told or commanded man to do. Reproduction is no exception. The feelings derived from the process of reproduction is the built in joy God gave to male and female for being obedient to his command. And no matter what you do or how you do it you will not top the joy built into the process; nor will you gain anything greater than what God provided in the process. Anyone thinking it is only fooling themselves. Sex, as used in everyday life is a bent, twisted term used to describe love, and is being portrayed as reproduction. Sex is not love! Love is not sex! Reproduction is not love. No where in the reproductive process did God mention love. Love exists with or without reproduction. Love is an indivisible unit existing in all mankind. It can't be divided into mother, father, sister, brother, or any other separate unit. It's whole; one unit. Trying to separate it is where the confusion comes in. God commanded us too love everybody; and we most certainly can do that.

## Jesus Provides For His People

Psalms 23:1

:1 The Lord is my shepherd; I shall not want.

I'm sure you've read the 23rd psalm many times, but did you ever stop to think the depth of the words and the assurance given to us by God? Look what it says: God is my keeper, I shall want for nothing. God is protecting me. He is looking out for my safety. He is watching for any danger that might head in my direction and He will prevent it from getting to me or doing me any harm. He is constantly looking out for greener pastures for me because he knows I'll need them as times goes on. He is constantly looking out for clean wholesome, calm waters for me to drink from. He wants the very best for me and constantly prepares for it so I will have it when it's needed. In short, God loves me, protects me, and provides for me.

When we look at this from our own perspective; the things we need daily to sustain life, the wisdom and knowledge needed to interact with people in a loving, caring, understanding and sharing way, we know that God is aware of our needs and provides those needs if we take the time to listen to His voice and remain obedience to His Word. What will happen to the sheep if they decide to ignore their shepherd and go off on their own, saying they can find their own pastures and drinking water? They will become subject to all the perils waiting to destroy them as soon as they leave the protection of the shepherd that can see troubles long before it reach them and lead them away, or around it.

That's what happens in so many cases. Some decide they can do it on their own and become disobedient to God's Word and ends up caught in the web of Satan who is out to destroy them.

God sees all of your needs and provides them. The answer to your needs is at your finger tips, but if you become blinded by Satan's lies, you can't see what God has provided.

## God's Word Will Get The Job Done

Isaiah 55:8-11

:8 For my thoughts are not your thoughts, neither are your ways my ways," says the Lord.

:9 For as the heavens are higher than the earth, so are my ways higher than your ways, and my thoughts than your thoughts

:19. For as the rain comes down, and snow from heaven and do not return there, but water the earth and make it bring forth and bud, that it may give seed to the sower, and bread to the eater,
:11 So shall my word be that goes forth of my mouth; it shall not return to me void, but it shall accomplish that which I please and it shall prosper in the thing Whereto I sent it.

First, let's look at one truth and undeniable fact: Jesus, throughout his ministry on earth, again and again, stated that: "The Father sent Me. John 1:1-4, In the beginning was the Word, and the Word was with God, and the Word was God. He was in the beginning with God. All things were made through Him, and without Him nothing was made that was made. In Him was life and the life was the light of men, Jesus is the Word, and God sent him to accomplish a purpose, which you know He did. God is saying to humanity that, whatever I say; My Word will do. He is also saying that Jesus is my prime example to you. Jesus repeated the same thing many times. "My Father sent me."

What it all means is; we can't rely on our own thinking and resolves when it comes to doing things God's way. The reason being, our thoughts, ideas and resolves are contaminated with humanity ways of doing things. Having learned these things our habits, attitudes and thinking are made up of them; that is, Satan's lies and deceptions. And these lies and deceptions become a way of life with us. So, God is warning us against these things. When we read and understand what Jesus did on earth, we know that he accomplished every item, deed, or task, God sent him to do. It's our example that God Word will accomplish its purpose.

Joseph Haugabrook

God is telling us plainly that his Word, as written in the bible, is for us to follow to the letter and without exceptions. When God gave Moses the words of the law, Moses had to write down exactly what God had said. When God gave Moses the measurements of the tabernacle and the Arc of the Covenant, Moses had to make all measurements exactly as God had stated. Whenever God told his prophets to say or do something they had to do it exactly as God had stated. There was a reason for that; only what God says will be effective. We can't add anything to it nor take anything away from it, if it is to work in our lives. You will note that God said, "My Word." Not anyone else. Not mine, yours, the preacher, deacon, president, governor, or anyone. It is what God says.

Jesus is still accomplishing, in our lives, everything God promised to us. But, whatever the words written in the holy bible say do, we have to do them the way the bible says do it. Let me give you and example: You say I love Sister Lula, or Brother John. But, I can't stand Sister Ellen, or Brother Willie. Well, I'll let you in on a little secret. You have just nullified love altogether. The reason; God Word does not give you the option of selective love. That is, loving who you choose and leaving out the rest. The thing God told you to hate and not love is sin. So, being selective is your way, not God's. And, the good things brought on by love will not happen in your life because you are not doing it God's way.

God prepared everything for us from the foundation of the earth, or from the beginning. It's done, it's over, God has completed all things for us. On the seventh day, God rested from all his work. The bible doesn't say he went back

66

to work after resting on the seventh day. So, everything we need has already been completed. The measurements are exact, the instructions are precise; and, are not going to change. God is not going to change things to fit our little ways, whether thinking or otherwise; we have to change our ways and thinking to fit what God have already put in place.

Jesus stated many times in the New Testament, that we are blessed. That means our blessing is already in place. But we have to follow the instructions in the bible to obtain them. In other words, our attitudes, actions, reactions, thinking, and interaction with people, places and things must be in accordance with the words in the bible.

We talked about this earlier but it bears mentioning again. Please remember God did not complicate things for us. He only gave us one thing to do: LOVE. When we let love become the driving force for our actions and deeds; that is, we do things for others because we want the very best for them, then we are fulfilling God's commandment. When Jesus told us "I give you a new commandment, love one another as I have loved you," he gave us the one thing that would guarantee us a prosper life on earth and eternal life with him. Our responsibility to God today is no more complicated than the commandment given to Adam in the Garden of Eden. There was one thing for Adam; there is one thing for us. For Adam, it was: "Don't eat of the tree in the midst of the garden." For us it is Love one another as I have loved you. Jesus loved us so much that he was willing, and did, take on the thing he hated; sin. It is worst than you having to put on clothes thoroughly covered with the worst kind of smelly dung. Jesus did it because he wanted the very best for us all.

The things written in the bible will be accomplished in our lives; it's up to us whether it will be blessings or curses. Blessing will come with obedience. Curses will come with disobedience. This is not a hell fire and brimstone scare, It's stating facts.

Remember you serve God by doing the things love is composed of: loving, being kind, helpful, and all the positives that make life better and more prosperous for all. Sure, you should sing, clap you hands, shout if you like; as long as you know, it's for your own edification, or outward expression, because you are so thankful to God for his blessing. Just know; doing these things is not what is required of you by commandment. You are not rewarded for those things, no more than a person walking by a music store will be paid by the store owner for stopping and dancing to the music. You are commanded by God to love. If you love, you will trust God, exercise your faith in him, believe and practice his word. These things you will be rewarded for.

Why Men Make Thing, Or Someone, Other Than Jesus, Their God

Isaiah 44:1 - 28 (Refer to the bible; read all 28 verses)

In this 44th chapter you note that God explained fully, man's intent, and its foolishness. Don't forget, we are looking at the people and their practices in the days of Isaiah.; And, as you read, you will also see that the practices of the people, in Malachi's day's, parallel our times and practices.; God sent his word to the people, through Isaiah, warning them of their practices and what they were doing to themselves by these beliefs and practices.; The people of the times, (Remember we are talking about the twelve tribes of Israel; God's chosen people) were making false gods and worshipping them. They were making images of wood, stone, and metals, and calling them their gods. Look at what God told them. "I am the only real God. I formed you in the womb and brought you forth into the world. I send you rain; I cause your seeds to sprout and spring up into bountiful harvests. In short God is letting them know that it's Him that is giving them life and life sustaining substances. The people were able to see by example what God was, and continued to do for those trusting his word. Then God explain the foolishness of their thinking and practices. He showed them how they go into the forest and get a tree. From that tree, he cooks his food, warm himself, make a tool or some other item; then he carve an image of a man or something else from that tree and call it his god; believing he can fall down and worship it and say to it deliver me, because I made you my god. How foolish is it to think that something that have no life, have no control of anything, not even itself, or it's existence, can perform some act, even a small one for you? Could the tree keep the man from cutting it down? Did the tree have any control of how it would be shaped or what it would be shape into? If the man so desired to shape it into a satanic figure the tree couldn't stop it. Nor could it stop the man from burning it entirely. But the man who cut down the tree had full control over what it would become; whether it was for heat, to cook food, or be shaped into an image; and named a god or something else. Man was in charge of its fate.

Note the word "control." Therein lies the thinking, practices and desires of man. Why do men shape an image from materials and call it a god? Why would man worship an image he has made and say to it deliver me? It's because man desires to be in control. I'm in control; I made you, I created you; you do what I say or I will destroy you! Man wants to be able to say that to his god. Man love the thought; "I may have made you my god, but don't let me have to remind you that you are my servant and will do what I say, when I say; because your continued existence is in my hands. In the minds of man, by making his own god, he is in control. In other words, by making his own god, man himself becomes the god; the almighty, the controller of destiny/fate.

The practice was foolish in Isaiah days just as it is today. And please, don't believe it's not going on just as strong right now as it was in the days of Isaiah. Yes, the styles may have changed over the years but the materials have not. Woods, minerals, stones, and metals are still being shaped and used to try and circumvent Gods control. Men still desire to be in control. Men still desire to control other men. They want the power to say, I hold the power of life or death over you. I decide whether you live or die; succeed or fail, become rich or live in poverty. I am the great I am. I am in control! Today, wealth and position, the things man has proclaimed to represent power and richer, are his gods. He can believe, in his mind, I put you on the pedestal and I can take you down. You represent power and riches because I gave you the title. But, just as I made you, I can break you.

So, man can sit back with enormous riches, in his high elected office and think "I'm in control, even though it's only in his mind. Yes, he's rich in man made wealth; he's president of the United States, but what control has he over his own life? He can't control, nor does he know whether he'll be alive the next second. Can he or his gods (man made richer and power) command rain in times of drought? Can he or his gods stop the rains bringing floods? Can he or his gods turn back the storms bearing down on his cities? What happens during these times? Well, he scramble to safety and hides from the storms. So, where are his or his god's controls?

Man attempting to circumvent God's power, was silly in earlier times and is more so today. Man's existence is in the hands of the true and living God. It was so in the beginning; it is so today. You are; because God is. Only God make true legends. Men are just legends in their own minds.

The Source Of Wisdom

James 1:5; Proverbs 2:6; 2Chronicles 1:10

:James 1:5 If any of you lack wisdom, let him ask of God, that giveth to all men liberally and upbraideth not; and it shall be given him.

:Proverbs 2:6 For the Lord giveth wisdom.

:2Chronicles 1:10 Give me now wisdom and knowledge

We know from the scriptures that wisdom comes from God; not age. And we'll further understand it as we talk more about wisdom.

The book of James tells us if you lack wisdom ask God. It further states, God will give it to you liberally, not just some measured amount that might not do the job. And he will not scold or chide you for asking.

We see the same thing in Proverbs 2:6. "For the Lord giveth wisdom: out of his mouth cometh knowledge and understanding." With knowledge and understanding we are able to execute righteous judgment. This is clearly shown in Solomon's Prayer; 2 Chronicles 1:10 "Give me now wisdom and knowledge." If wisdom came through age why wasn't Solomon asking for long life so he would be able to gain knowledge to rule God's people. And why those, much older that Solomon, sought out his wisdom? The reason is not difficult; look at Job 32:9 (it bears reading the entire 32nd chapter) "Great men are not always wise: neither do the aged understand judgment." Elihu was talking to a man (Job) much older than he. At first, Elihu was afraid to speak his opinion because he was like many people today. He believed wisdom came with age. In other words, what can I, a young man tell this person who is old? Looking at God's response to Solomon's prayer, he didn't say, ok Solomon, I know wisdom should come with age, but I'm going to make an exception and give it to you now. Neither did he say I'm going to give you long life so you can gain wisdom. God gave him, first of all, wisdom far above others. And, he gave him riches, long life, and honor.

If we want to put age in the process it can only fit in one place: Age, or long life, comes as a result of wisdom. It's important to remember that God, not the experiences gained through trials and errors, give wisdom. You are precious to Jesus Christ and he will give you more than what you need to live, according to His Word. You will not be without understanding in your action and interaction with people. Ask him how to conduct your life in a Godly manner; you'll be surprise at the benefits that comes with it.

## The Danger Of Man's Wisdom

Corinthians 2:1-5

:1 And I brethren, when I came to you, came not with Excellency of speech or of wisdom, declaring unto you the testimony of God.

:2 For I determined not to know anything among you, save Jesus Christ, and him crucified.
:3 And I was with you in weakness, and in fear, and in much trembling.

:4 And my speech and my preaching was not with enticing words of man's wisdom but in demonstration of the Spirit and of power;

:5 That your faith should not stand in the wisdom of men, but in the power of God.

Look closely at what the Word of God is saying to us through Paul. Paul didn't go to the Corinthians speaking of worldly things which is easily grasped and readily accepted by people in general. He didn't speak in ways to entice or motivate people to act on his words, as many were doing at the time, and in this present time, for personal gain. Paul was using what many at the time thought of as foolish words. Paul was preaching hope in Jesus Christ, which for many, who couldn't see how anything Paul preached could occur; was foolishness. They didn't see Jesus, they didn't know him, so how could they believe in something they couldn't see, feel, or know existed; nor had the leaders and scholars of the time affirmed? And yet, Jesus was what Paul was preaching to them. And, he was doing it in the spirit which made it even harder for them to grasp, because, unless you are spiritual it is impossible to discern the things of the Spirit. In other words you have to be spiritual in order to understand the Word and hope in Christ Jesus. In hope you don't see the things you desire, but you believe that the Words of Jesus are true and will be manifested as written. The Hebrew boys didn't see themselves being saved from the fiery furnace when they stood at the top being prepared to be thrown in; but they believed that God would save them. In other words, their hope of being saved from the flames was in God. Daniel didn't see himself being saved from the hungry lions, but his hope of being saved was in God. Hope is not having something in your hand, but believing it exist, and, that Jesus has it in his hands and will deliver it to you. To see, taste, or smell it before believing is not hope; it's not even believing; it just accepting that; what I see, smell or taste is what it says it is.

Having to have something physically available to be seen, touched, smelled or tasted, is man's wisdom and knowledge, and the danger in that is; it takes you out of believing and having faith in Jesus Christ. The bible today is still foolishness to many because they would rather believe what man says than what God has recorded in his Holy Bible.

Paul is saying to the Corinthians, "I didn't come to you trying to make myself great, I came in meekness, making us all the same and showing you the truth in Christ Jesus through the demonstration of the power of Jesus Christ. Not my power but the power of Jesus Christ. Unless it is taught and preached in accordance with the bible, it is not of Jesus Christ, but tradition, and trickery of men. Man's wisdom and knowledge takes you out of the wisdom and knowledge of Jesus Christ.

Again, it's often said that wisdom comes with age. And, when it comes to man's wisdom I will not dispute that. But look at one example. If wisdom is a product of age, then the doctors, talking with Jesus in the temple, when he was twelve years old, would not have had the reaction they had to his questions and answers. And look at Luke 21:15, "For I will give you a mouth and wisdom, which all your adversaries shall not be able to gainsay nor resist." Understanding God's word and applying it to daily life is not a function of age but a revelation from God.

With man, there is a limit to his understanding of things around him. Children, as they grows into adulthood, understand better why their parents told them not to do certain things, like smoke, drink, or engage in certain activities. They understand it mainly because they experience certain negative effects from it, in addition to seeing others experience the same. On the flip side, they see the good being derived from doing the right thing, and understand why their parents stressed doing right. In this example, wisdom becomes a product of age because the understanding is event driven. It's like citizens urging city leaders to put up a stop light or stop sign at certain spots because of the danger it poses. The city fathers only act when someone is killed or seriously injured. Their inaction was a lack of knowledge of the problems and burdens this spot would lead to.

It only take a quick glance into society to see that a vast number of people are depending on those who have gained their knowledge through the political arena or institutions that, in many cases, do not believe in God to solve their individual, family, community and national problems. Man is depending on man to solve his problem; and therein lies the great misunderstanding. And yes, it does takes time for man to grow into an understanding of people, places and things, because events occur with time. But remember; with the existence of mass confusion, man may never sort-out what is real or true. Why do you think Jesus says plainly, lean not to your own understanding. It's because we know in part, we understand in part, and unless we see the whole picture, our decisions and actions are based on "in part" understanding. Truth is; Jesus knows everything about everything. He made us, and the world. He knows when we will be born and when we will pass from this world into the next. He knows every word we will speak and with what attitude we will speak it. He knows our every need, and desire. He knows every atom making up every cell in our bodies, and the universe. He knows every path out feet will take and orbit the planets follows. He knows every thought our minds will develop or entertain; and this doesn't begin to scratch the surface. So, to understand these things fully we have to see them in their entirety. To be able to help a person gain strength you have to have a full understanding of his weakness. And since you; man; see and understand in part, how you can understand fully without a revelation from Jesus; who has the full picture in view.

Man, today, is flapping around like a sheet in the wind trying to find solutions to the plaguing problems of society. For teen pregnancy; he offers condoms. For drug and alcohol addiction; he's offering a verbal "say no." For crime; he's offering more and larger jails, and the some cases, death by "so called" legal means. Because man is leaning on his own wisdom; that is, the knowledge gained through man's experiences; problems and the magnitude of them grows worse in the world daily.

Wisdom is given by Jesus Christ, and he puts no age restriction on it. We understand the Word of God by a revelation from Jesus Christ. If you seek an understanding of His Word, it doesn't matter how young or old you are, He will give it to you. And when He gives it, it's not going to be based on your age. And it will not be an understanding for just one, or one age group; with another understanding for another; it will be the same for all. Remember, Satan will throw a confusion factor in your search for understanding if you, in anyway, let your ego get into the picture. That's why Paul said: "And I, brethren, when I came to you came not with Excellency of speech or of wisdom, declaring unto you the testimony of God. For I determined not to know anything among you, save Jesus Christ and him crucified. He did not let self get in the picture; and neither should we. We should never forget; wisdom is one of our great gifts from Jesus Christ.

Some refer to the two as; Spiritual Wisdom and worldly wisdom. If you want to use it that way, it's ok, just as long as you know wisdom gained through man's trials and errors, is not wisdom revealed by Jesus Christ.

## Don't Let Your Wisdom Be A Stumbling Block

I Corinthians 1:18-25

:18  For the preaching is to them that perish foolishness; but unto us which are saved it is the power of God.

:19  For it is written; I will destroy the wisdom of the wise and bring to nothing the understanding of the prudent.

:20  Where is the wise? Where is the scribe? Where is the disputer of this world? Has not God made foolish the wisdom of this world?

:21  For after that in the wisdom of God the world by wisdom knew not God, it pleased God by the foolishness of preaching to save them that believe.

:22  For Jews request a sign, and Greeks seek after wisdom;

:23    But we preach Christ crucified, unto the Jews a stumbling block and to the Greeks foolishness,

:24    But to unto them which are called, both Jews and Greeks, Christ the power of God, and the wisdom of God.

:25   Because the foolishness of God is wiser than men, and the weakness of God is stronger than men

Jesus is pointing out clearly and simply that it is important to understand what he says about how we are to conduct ourselves in this life on earth. Jesus wants us to understand his teaching as to how we should interact with people and things in every function we perform each day. God's way of doing things is so far above the way man do things that man don't understand them and thus brand them foolishness, pipe dreams, and other meaningless terms. I don't have to tell you, just look into any community and see how man is abandoning God's way for the ways of men. Even in church, where the bible is preached, each week, the ways of men have invaded the pulpit, Sunday school, and other areas of the congregation. Being politically correct has become more important than being spiritually correct. The big difference in God's ways over man's ways; God ways filter out sins; corruptions, envy, hatred, greed, lusts, addictions, murder, adultery, to name a few. In man ways, these things filters through and are covered up, or made to look like a normal function of life, by developing catchy terms and words that sounds good and proper. However, God's way places truth before men; a fact that cannot be denied. Man's ways paints false pictures and egos builders before men; things suited to their lusts and evil desires.

These two differences make God's ways and man's ways opposite of each other. Look in any society today; mean, evil acts are called "pranks" Sexual immorality are called "being normal and healthy." Abomination is called "alternative life styles." and accepted as just another way God gave man to live his life. There are so many examples that I could never cite them all here; but, in the end, the right way is what God says in his Holy bible.

To summarize what Jesus is saying to us in these verses; I have already completed the big picture and each part you see and live are but tiny parts of what I have already completed. You, man, can only see the tiny part you live each day. Therefore, if you reject the part I have given to you, and make up a part on your own, and try to fit it into what I already have in place, it will not work. You can't develop something to fit into something you don't have the slightest idea of what it is, or what it will look like in the end. In other words how can you develop a piece to fit in a puzzle that you don't have the slightest idea of what the whole puzzle will look like when it's finished. It is silly to look at a piece of a puzzle and reject it, saying that piece is not right, especially when you have no idea of what the completed puzzle will be. Jesus never hindered us from gaining wisdom and knowledge, he wants us to have it; just don't use it to try and change what Jesus already have in place.

Let's Talk About Jesus

Isn't There A Solution To The Problems Of The Nations?

Jeremiah 8:22

:22  Is there no balm in Gilead, is there no physician there? Why then is not the health of the daughter of my people recovered?

The nations have a problem. They attempt to change the Word of God to fit the terms invented by man to justify his deeds in the name of modernity. Things God said are abominable, man has decided to make them right and good by using the term politically correct. It may be political correct; meaning "right in the eyes of man" but it's only in man's eyes; not God.

In the late 1980's my wife and I drove through a small town in Arkansas (this town is not unique, the same thing exist in most towns in America) and counted the number of churches in a four block area. There were four churches; each had signs with words designed to lure attendees. However, spending just over a week in the town and talking with people; we found what exist there, existed in a lot of American towns; large and small. We found; racial hatred and separation; false pride and over inflated egos. Teen pregnancy, drug and alcohol addictions, men and women exploiting youth sexually, some churches offering dating services, corrupt politicians and law enforcement officers, schools knowingly teaching false information, families being torn apart by government intervention in child rearing. Parents doing bodily harm to children because of the government turning proper child rearing into child abuse;

frustrating parents to the point of over reacting, and the list goes on. So, where is the church in all this? It's being politically correct, because the words of men have dictated it. It is more popular to be politically correct, because it is where the money is; and the officials of the church have decided, and convinced the congregations, that it is more beneficial financially, to the church body to change their thinking and practices to fit's man developed terms than the Word of God. It's like going to a warehouse that sells unclaimed boxes. You don't know what's in the box until you buy it. Congregations get caught up in this deception; not knowing what the end results will be; and, that it is against God's Word.

God didn't give the responsibility of child rearing to politicians to legislate. God didn't give the responsibility of morality to the politicians to legislate. Child rearing was left to parents and morality to men God called to lead his people. The leaders of God's people have dropped the ball. Churches are offering everything but the Word of God to solve Family and community problems. Can you imagine a pastor and church officials bringing in counselors, of different sorts, to counsel it members on family and community problems? The same counselors being brought in live among these members; and the problems listed above are still running rampart in the community. So, why turn to those living in the midst of the problem and cannot solve the ones touching their own lives? It's the same as seeing a bunch of people, who can't swim, caught in rapids and throwing in those who also can't swim, to save them.

Is there no balm in Gilead? The word of God is everywhere. So, yes there is balm in Gilead; but it's not being used; man has turned to man for answers to his problems. In other words, the chickens have turned to the fox for protection from the fox.

Is there no physician there? Well that is questionable; because money, sex, and life pleasures are corrupting so many people that "modern leaders of God's people" seem to be playing; what's my line. Being a Pastor has become more of give me my price and I'll say what you want me to say, rather than I'll stand on God's Word regardless."

## There Is A Solution To Present Day Problems

Mark: 10:28-30

:28 Then Peter began to say unto him, Lo, we have left all and have followed thee.

:29 And Jesus answered and said, Verily I say unto you, There is no man that hath left house, or brethren, or sisters, or father, or mother, or wife, or children,, or lands, for my sake, and the gospel's,

:30 But he shall receive an hundredfold now in this time, houses, an brethren, and sisters, and mothers, and children, and lands, with persecutions; and in the world to come eternal life.

Speaking from experience I can truly say that many

harbors' Peter type thinking. Many years ago, I felt the same way. I didn't want to give up what I thought was fun; drinking, chasing females, night clubbing, and the like. To me I was having the time of my life. I felt that fun only came through the life I was living. And if I changed, and lived like my pastor, parents and some others were trying to get me to do; I would be giving up the things worth living for. But, my life did change. As my earlier teaching; in my home and church, began setting in, I started to see that what I had been told was really what mattered in life. I began seeing and understanding that it was not how many homes a man break up that matters, it's how many he help keep together. It's not how many women a man exploit, but how many he helps to become faithful, loving mates. It's not how much alcohol a man can drink, but how little he can live happily without. It's not the amount of revelry, but the amount of peaceful resolve that matters. It's very easy to get caught up in the predominant ways around you. And, with so many things, existing in communities that are not conducive to Godly living; many people are being overwhelmed by them.

Men and women, for different reasons, fall prey to ways in violation of God's commandments. The main reason is peer pressure; wanting to be accepted by the group; or sometimes; maybe, just another person. Many bad deeds have been committed because someone wanted to be liked by another. Many evils have been committed because someone truly believed that what they were doing was the only way to get what they wanted out of life.

What are the facts; what is truth? Well, the reality of it all is: the Words spoken by Jesus in the 29th and 30th verse are true. Follow the teaching of Jesus, believe and have faith in his Word and you will have far more of the things that you want than you ever thought possible. A person seeking enjoyment may call it fun, pleasure, and many other given names. In reality they are seeking to satisfy a longing or desire that's driving them from one thing to another. Today it's drinking, tomorrow it's something else; drugs, adultery, crime, and the list goes on. The yearning is never satisfied because they find no real satisfaction; because satisfaction can only come from good, or truth. Short term appeasement can be derived from things, other than good or truth but it's just that; short term appeasement; not a lasting fulfillment.

When you become satisfied, there is no longer a yearning, or desire for something else. You may desire to do more, because of the great satisfaction derived from seeing the results of you act. I've seen young boys and girls change from being disrespectful to excellent examples of respect, because of one act of kindness. like one kid helping an old lady pick up groceries that had fallen from a torn bag and scattered all over the streets. He not only carried the groceries home for her, he began helping elderly people in his and other communities; cutting grass free, and doing what repairs he could around their homes. He no longer found it enjoyable to poke fun at old people. But, he did find great joy in helping them.

Health, peace of mind and sprit, and yes, wealth, is found in doing good things for others. Planting good seeds will results in harvesting good fruits. Leave the things that are making you violate the commandments of Jesus and you will be rewarded with an abundance of the things you really want in this life; and the life to come.

## People Of God Settling Their Differences Among Themselves

### Corinthians 6:1-5

:1 Dare any of you, having a matter against another, go to the law before the unjust, and not before the saints.

:2 Do you not know the saints shall judge the world? and if the world shall be judge by you, are ye unworthy to judge the smallest matters?

:3 Know ye not that we shall judge angels? how much more things that pertain to this life?

:4 If then ye have judgments of things pertaining to this life, set them to judge who are least esteemed in the church.

:5 I speak to your shame. Is it so, that there is not a wise man among you? No, not one that shall be able to judge between his brethren?

The scriptures given here are; short, sweet, and to the point. Jesus is telling us through Paul that we should not turn to the unjust to judge our concerns in a righteous manner. To put it another way, we should not turn to the devil to get Godly advice. It's like looking for truth in a lie; or, looking for holiness in sin.

Jesus is telling us that we, who are practicing his teaching; that is, obeying his word; should, because we can, settle differences between us instead of going to courts. When two saints go to court to settle a difference, they have abandoned the teaching of Jesus and turned to the practices of men. They have pushed aside righteous and took on unrighteous ways.

Since this lesson is so clear, I'll end by saying, no matter what the difference is, it can be settled through using and practicing God's Word. If we say we are saints, why are we using the unjust to settle differences? The courts, small and large, are overwhelmed with cases of fights between individuals; the vast majority being saints against saints; or, church going folks against church going folks. Where is our faith in Jesus? Do you actually believe it can be dropped and picked up at will? As Paul said; shame on you for using the unjust to judge righteously.

## Shall Affliction Be A Worry

Psalms 34:17-19

:17 The righteous cry and the Lord heareth and delivereth them out of all their troubles.

:18 The Lord is nigh unto them that are of a broken heart;

and saveth such as be of a contrite spirit.

:19 Many are the afflictions of the righteous: but the Lord delivereth him out of them all.

Should afflictions indeed be a worry? Putting it another way, and on a personal basis; should I worry about the conditions that confronts me, sometimes daily, causing hardships and heartaches. Should I worry about the utility bill being so high I can't pay it all this month? Should I worry about not having the money to pay my rent, or mortgage; or something I'm depending on breaking down, or will not function? Should I worry about that close family member being in trouble with a habit, or the law? Should these and many others that may confront me be a worry; or an opportunity to test my faith?

There was this runner that wanted to be a track star. His conversations and daily activities centered on what he wanted to be. One day he declared himself fit and capable (and indeed he was) of accomplishing what he wanted to do. He was then pitted in a race with other strong, healthy athletes; his great opportunity to test his ability. But, fear set in, causing doubt; and his defeat; rendering his ability naught. The young man was fast, his clock time; with no competition; set a record. He was truly capable of beating the competition; but, he failed. It was not what he faced that defeated him, it was the weight of fear he placed on his shoulders.

Jesus has already told us afflictions will come. We know up front when we determine within ourselves that we are going to live a righteous life that the adversary is going to try every trick in the book to defeat us. He is not going to sit on the sideline and let you run without competition. Many sportsmen, or sport teams will try to demoralize their opponents before going in the arena, knowing that if they can break the opponent's spirit they will become easy prey.

Jesus gives us every assurance that we will be victorious over all that comes against us; including; ills of all kinds; troubles, sickness, financial, physical, mental and all else. But we have to use the tool he gave us to do it; faith. How                                                                                                    did, Daniel survive the lion den? How did the Hebrew boys survive the fiery furnace?

And many other acts of faith that's too numerous to mention; it was through exercising faith, rather that succumbing to fear. It took me a long time to jump a cross bar higher that four feet because fear told me before I took the first step toward it; you'll never make it. It was only when I said; it's possible that I did. Jesus tells us to have faith. That tells me my victory lies in faith. According to your faith be it unto you. If you think you can't; you can't. If you think you can, you can.

Will there be afflictions? Yes, they will come in the form of family, community, national and universal ills and problems. Should they be a worry? No, because worrying kills faith. Yes, you are faced with it and must do something about it, but you will not let worrying be a part of your actions. Jesus is telling us here, the same thing God told Moses at the Red Sea; "Stretch out your Rod." The Rod represented faith, and Moses stretched out faith and brought the power of God into action and the sea was parted. When we stretch out on faith, we activate the power of Jesus Christ; and who, or what, can overcome the power of Jesus. Strong bridges will span the rapids that try to engulf you. A guiding light will appear leading you safely out of darkness. Your needs, whatever they are, will be met. Never mind the fact, you already have that overbearing gas bill, or eviction notice in hand; or whatever problem that's upon you, Jesus is saying to you I see and understand your needs, but my hands are tied unless you use the tool I've given you. You are fit and able; don't let the burden of fear prevent you from being victorious. Afflictions are not barriers that can't be overcome; they are opportunities to use your faith. That's what makes the 19th verse reality; the righteous will use their faith.

### Let nothing Steal Your God Given Joy

Psalm 118:24

:24 This is the day which the Lord hath made; We will rejoice and be glad in it.

This morning when I woke up, even though it was 21 degrees outside, a bird, I think was a mocking bird, was singing. I mentioned to my wife that it was a little odd that a bird was singing in such cold weather. And you must admit this is not the norm. My wife's response, however, brought a jolting reality. Outside near where the bird was singing, is an area where we feed birds, a wide variety of birds eat the sorted variety of seed we put out for them. Her response was, "The birds are thankful for the food area." Cold, a heavy frost, the type thing that make birds puff themselves and seek as much cover as possible from the elements; yet this bird was singing.

Look at the verse above. This is the day the Lord has made. We will rejoice and be glad in it. What is better than waking up in the morning and knowing there is a place where all your daily needs can be fulfilled.

We have, through Jesus Christ, access to a great variety of solutions God has provided to fulfill, even our desires. I like to compare it to a strong hungry fellow standing near a table spread with all kinds of good looking, good smelling and good tasting foods ready to be eaten. But, between him and the table is a little scrawny, weak, toothless fellow with nothing more than a loud voice daring him to take food from the table. Putting yourself in the strong man's position, the question become, am I going to let this little fellow, whom I can shove aside any time I choose, stop me from taking the food I need to live? He has no weapon against my strength, not even teeth to bite; so, am I going to let him turn me away, or am I going to use my strength to shove him aside, take what has been provided for me, eat, live and rejoice that my needs are met? I think you get the picture.

We have the solutions, and the variety to fulfill our every need. However, there are many things that will try to prevent us from obtaining our needs in life. We are faced with many problems of life; such as family problems, being lied on, cheated in finances, lost of jobs, transportation problems, lack of finance for urgent needs and the list goes on. And yes, your particular situation may, at times, seem hopeless. Reality is; the situation is never hopeless. God, through Jesus have provided us a way to successfully overcome any situation. The thing to do is, first of all, have faith in Jesus that regardless of the situation facing you there is a place to get the solution you need. So, in sincerity, you pray for the solution, believing as you pray that Jesus will provide what you are asking for. If you've ever used a Polaroid camera, you know when you first snap the picture and the camera pushes out the film, there was nothing on it but a blank space. You saw nothing, yet you had the faith when you snapped the picture that the image you snapped would appear on that piece of film the camera pushed out. And, as you held the film the scene you snapped slowly become the image you wanted to capture.

As you pray in faith, the thing you are praying for may not be visible at the moment, but with your faith you know it will materialize, and it will, just like the picture on the film. This is why God want us, through Jesus Christ, to rejoice each and every day. What he is saying to us through this scripture; I have given you the means, the guidance and the power to reach out and take what you need from the table I have spread for you. Don't just wait for sunny days, when things are going well, to rejoice, rejoice regardless of the weather or condition. Every day is a day to smile, be helpful, sharing, understanding, loving, and exercise faith and hope. I've brought you into another day; rejoice that I've filled it with all the goodness of my love for you. I am with you, I will never leave you. I see your needs, I've provided for them; all you have to do is follow the guide lines I've given to you.

As you go through your daily tasks; think about the bird singing on a cold frosty morning. Someone may think it's odd for you to be happy and smiling because conditions around you normally dictates that you should be otherwise. But, you are not affected by conditions thrown at you by the world. Your faith is in Jesus, who have provided the atmosphere for your happiness; an atmosphere the world may not understand, but you do. You know you are strong enough to push the scrawny little fellow aside and eat. You rejoice, are happy, and smile, regardless of the worldly conditions around you. You know God made this day; gave you life in it and want you to be happy and thankful in it.

Don't Worry About Others; Just Trust In The Lord And Do Good.

Psalm 37:1-4

:1 Fret not thyself because of evildoers, neither be thou envious against the workers of iniquity.

:2 For they shall soon be cut down like the grass, and wither as the green herb.

:3 Trust in the Lord, and do good; Dwell in the land and verily thou shalt be fed.

:4 Delight thyself also in the Lord, and he shall give thee the

Joseph Haugabrook

desires of thine heart.

God is saying that as you go about earning your daily bread, (the necessities of life; food, shelter, clothing and the likes) you will encounter a variety of attitudes, personalities, thinking, actions, reactions and all the things that make up the individuals you will interact with. Don't let how these individuals live their lives determine how you will live yours. It doesn't matter whether a person is doing good or evil, his or her ways should not determine your ways. If you do good because another person is doing good, you are on the wrong track. It's like driving in the same ruts as a car ahead of you; your tires will hit everything the lead car tires hit. Your life should not be patterned after another person, but rather after the Word of God. Even the prophets and disciples taught the people to look to God; look to Jesus Christ. Why was this a constant theme? Remember Jesus response when he was called good. "There is none good but the Father." Jesus was in the flesh and flesh has to stay in the Word 24/7, from birth to death, in order to be good. Revelation tells us that Jesus was the only one worthy to open the seven seals, because he was the only one who was in the flesh and remained in the Word 24/7 from birth to death. The flesh is weak and subject to fall at any time without the strength of Jesus Christ. Therefore Jesus is telling us now, don't get upset over the deeds of others. Don't worry because it seems you are struggling while doing good to earn your daily bread and the person working next to you steals, lies, cheats and worse, and has plenty of money and other things in his or her possession. That is the wrong thing to keep your eyes on. Amassing wealth through wrong doing is the same as building your house on a cliff that is prone to bad erosion during heavy rains. It is only a matter of time until the heavy rains come. And for sure will come, and there goes your house.

The bible is our guide through this life for safe arrival with Jesus in the life to come. Read the bible; learn what it is saying to you. Listen attentive to those speaking in accordance to the bible dictates. That is, showing in words what the bible is telling you to do in your interactions with others. And don't worry; if you sincerely seek the truth Jesus will not let anyone lead you to destruction. Don't worry if you transform your mind; to be satisfied with the things Jesus told you to be satisfied with, Jesus will give you the desires of your heart. It's simple, first things first. You will have the money to pay those bills. You will have that new home, car, furniture, vacation and other things; why? Because your thinking, actions and reactions are never evil but good. Your intentions are not to brag, look big, be important, or some other vain reason; you want it to enjoy in this life without any fore thought of malice. There is a path to the store house of blessings but you must follow the path Jesus paved to reach it.

What Should I Do?

(Troubles)

For just a while; concentrate on: Trouble.

Joseph Haugabrook

Behind me I see trouble following closely

On either side I see trouble walking alongside me.

In front of me I see trouble just one step ahead.

Sound familiar? These are not just idle words. They are feelings/emotions and attitudes that creates hopelessness and mental suffering that has, is, and will, drive many to extreme measures; some to take their own life.

If this overwhelming feeling come upon you; what are you to do? Is there a remedy for an extreme need for food, clothing and shelter? Can a father or mother wake up in the morning and find an answer to the cry of their hungry child? Or, that eviction notice being carried out that very day? Or that notice that says you are now unemployed? Is there a solution; something that will provide hope and assurance for such negatives?

I refer you to the Word of God. I will not refer you to a particular scripture, because many times that is more of a hindrance than help when it comes to relying on the Word of God. I am not pointing a finger at anyone, but the trend is to get a particular scripture, one we feel will address our need, or condition and read it, without giving any thought to our own actions up to and including that very moment. Our efforts should be to learn the Word of God in its entirety. Getting to know God's Word is to build trust and faith in Him; which will give us the necessary information needed for our own role in receiving His promises.

This modern age teaches that everything should be instantaneous, or very fast. We want to be at our destination before we leave the starting point. We want dinner done before it starts cooking. We want everything yesterday. We want a so-called-expert or professional to tell us how to rear out children; how to stop being sassed or hit by our children. How to stop addictions, teen pregnancy; and the list goes on. We elect officials studded with moral weaknesses, with the expectation that their efforts will bring about moral strength. In other words, in nearly everything, we look to moral weakness, hoping to find morale strength. And because we do; there's trouble; behind, along side and ahead of us. So, what are we to do?

First and foremost, don't look for specific scriptures to cover a specific condition or event at the time it is occurring or is upon you. It's like sitting around with your house unlocked or unprotected and a burglar comes in and over powers you; and, at that moment, you start searching for something you think can turn the tide in your favor. You are not sure but you think you have something that might work, because you've heard, from others, that it would. This type thinking is: "why not try it; things can't get any worse than this." But, they can without the proper preparation; that is, understanding the word of God.

Conditions comes upon us for many reasons; some resulting from our own actions, some from the actions of others. But, regardless of the reason there is a solution to the ill plaguing mankind; and it's found in understanding and practicing the teachings of Jesus Christ. It doesn't matter whether trouble is behind, alongside, or in front of you; Jesus is always between you and trouble if you follow his Word. Yes, you may see trouble and it may appear to be covering you, but look close enough and you'll see that Jesus is holding it at bay; as long as you are following his instructions. However, if you choose to ignore his instructions trouble may very well cover you; because you are pushing away the very help you need to protect you.

I can't begin to mention all the ills facing mankind everyday; nor is it important to mention them. The important thing is read, understand and practice the teachings of Jesus Christ every day. Don't try to find quick fixes in the bible for problems, facing you. Read the bible as often as possible. Understand, or seek understanding for what you read. And, most important, practice what you read and understand. Let your interaction with people, places and things be exactly as the bible outlines. If you look back to the Old Testament, our examples of God working among mankind; we'll see that the servants of God didn't wait until trouble faced them to try and learn about God; they followed his Word in all of their interactions. Daniel didn't wait until he was thrown in the lion's den. The Hebrew boys didn't wait until they were being thrown in the fiery furnace they lived the word daily.

Read, learn, and practice the Word of God. Read the whole bible; stop just picking scriptures that you feel will cover what you are experiencing at the moment.

Yes, you will see trouble all around you; and it may seem too close for comfort. But, if you follow Jesus Christ instructions you will walk away from trouble unharmed.

Let's Talk About Jesus

Impatience

For a while concentrate on: Impatience

First, look at the reality of the word. Impatience is: the inability to control one's desire for action; "can't wait; in too much of a hurry."

Changing customs and habits have twisted and turned thinking, actions and reactions into deeds of impatience and indecision. Action and reaction toward everything that governs life has been put on a fast moving assemble line. Everything must be done now; I have to have it now. I must see it manifested now. I don't have the luxury of waiting. It takes too long; I left because the line was too long. Church services are just too long; and the list goes on. (Moving, skipping, hopping but nothing is being done)

This same thinking attitudes and actions are being applied to the most important thing in life; saving the soul. Take this thinking for instant; wanting different scriptures to read each day. The great evil in this type thinking is hopping from scripture to scripture without doing what the first one say do. What the use reading different scriptures when what the first one said is not being followed. What's happening is; the reader feels good, because even though what is being read on Monday is not followed, there is a new one to read on Tuesday, Wednesday, Thursday and etc. It's like, well I didn't do everything the Word said on Monday, but it's ok, I'll try Tuesday's verse. In this case the end result is nothing, except reading is being accomplished. It's like the story told by a preacher. His deacon came to him and said; Reverend, you have preached the same sermon for a whole month now, the people are talking; when are you going to change it? The preacher asked the deacon had he done everything the sermon said should be done. When the deacon answered no; the preacher said; well, when you do everything the sermon says do then I'll change it. Read one scripture until you understand and practice it before moving on; that is growing in the Word. Wanting change is not what's needed. Understanding and doing what God says do, is what's needed. Changing scriptures are not the answer. Sticking with one until it is understood and applied to life is the answer.

Read this scripture until it become a part of your life; Luke 21:19. Look also at verse 14-18, as it points out conditions of life. This verse shows how important patience is; and what good thing it will accomplish.

Impatience can cause many negative things. For instant, Genesis 19:4-9 shows how it causes lust. Genesis 34:25-27 shows how it brings on revenge. And Genesis 25:29-34 shows how it causes the loss of things precious. Numbers 20:10-12 shows how the children were kept out of the promise land. And Job 2:7-9 shows how a foolish statement can easily be made. Of course there are much more, but the point is, being impatience causes flip flop in practicing the teaching of God. I ask you to read the scriptures of patience, and practice it until it becomes second nature to you; whether it takes one day, or one year. Again, it's not how much you read, but rather how much you understand. (This is not saying don't read the entire bible, you should; just understand as you go.)

Let's Talk About Jesus

Luke 21:19 shows what can be accomplished through patience. Genesis, Numbers and Job shows what happens when patience is pushed aside.

Train Up A Child In The Way He Should Go

Proverbs 22:6

:6 Train up a child in the way he should go: and when he is old, he will not depart from it.

Certain times of year; like holidays; especially Christmas; a lot of emphasis will be placed on children, in all walks of life. Special feelings and emotions will be displayed in their behalf. Many will befriend a child they don't know and in all probability, will never know, or even see again. This effort, in turn, creates a special feeling of love and joy in what might have been a sad child during this period. Over the years these feelings and emotions have been learned taught and practiced as traditional. Tradition says this is a time of joy and peace. Tradition says this is a time of giving and receiving. So, to live up to tradition, we somehow find this inner joy and make efforts to spread it around. Don't think I'm knocking giving, receiving, joy and peace; God forbid. The point I'm making is; the way we celebrate certain seasons comes from what has been taught, learned and practiced. Kids are taught; for instant; that Santa Claus loves them and gives them toys. Later, when the kids learn it was really mom and dad doing the giving, because they loved them, the giving parts that were taught remains. So, from the beginning, giving and being happy about it, was taught and the teaching stays with the kids into adulthood. The kid, once grown, gives to their kids and so it goes.

Train a child in the way he should go; this is the responsibility placed on parents by God. God, in his holy word, gave directions for proper training. And, if followed, will lead to a God fearing, law abiding child that will take the training into adulthood and thus train his or her child.

Please, pay close attention to the first three words: Train a child. God is commanding us to train our children. But, from that point on God leaves it up to us how the child will be raised. God let us look at our own child and say; I want my child to be: whatever you want it to be. And, from that point on it becomes your decision. You decide if you want the child to be good or bad. (Note, the scriptures do not consider or address man developed professions; it deals with good, bad, morality, immorality; accepting, practicing the Word of God; or not accepting it.) If you want your child to be God-fearing, loving, kind, respectful, cooperative, understanding, sharing and interact with people in a loving, sharing way at all times, then that is what you should teach; starting at an early age. Now, look at the rest of the phrase. "The way he should go." You know full well that you can't raise a child to shoplift and expect him or her to go in a store filled with eye catching goods and not shoplift. Ma barker couldn't expect her sons to be law abiding when she had raised them to be lawbreakers.

What the scriptures is telling us; we have a choice of how we want to raise and train our children. But, we have to keep one thing in mind; how we raise, or let them be raised, is the way they will be, even into adulthood. God has given us the assurance, that what we instill in the child is going o remain in him or her. And we will be the recipient of what we raised. Also, we are held responsible for the way our children are raised. We are given the right way to do it, but we are given the option of accepting or rejecting that way. God does not force his Word on anyone, he gives us the option of accepting or rejecting it. Just remember, God gives us fair warning, that the bridge we build is the bridge we will cross.

If we choose to ignore the Word of God, be it known, God is not mocked. If God said it will come to pass; it will. I can't emphasize this too strongly; God put the responsibility of raising each child squarely on the shoulders of parents. I don't care what the government says; parents should raise children without interference from governments. The only way to raise up God fearing, loving, kind, respectful, caring, sharing children, with high morals, is to start early, and just as you teach Christmas, teach them the ways of love. The great part about this is; God tells us how to do it and what the outcome will be. Look at your child right now. The seeds you are planting in his mind today will become the fruit that will be reaped in later years.

## Lest We Forget

Proverbs 10:12

:12 Hatred stirs up strife, but love covers all sins.

Take one food item that you like very much. No matter how much you like it or how many times you've eaten it; if you didn't know the truth about it, in the back of your mind you would always have questions like; is it bad for me? Will it cause some kind of negative reaction in my body? I love it but should I really be eating it? And the list goes on. Thing is, you don't have complete trust in it; and that which you don't have complete trust in you don't love. In modern times; we have substituted "love" with; "tolerance." And tolerance is; putting up with something, because you have to. Why? It's the politically correct, thing to do; and, at the same time, hide your true feelings and beliefs. When love (Wanting the very best for another and putting forth the efforts to make it happen) is applied the gaping wounds of mistrust and unknowns are completely covered with truth and reality. And, unless truth and reality is the guiding force in your interaction with people, places and things, your efforts are void of love, thereby providing a path for the negatives of life to control your emotions, actions and reactions.

The importance of our subject is; we sometimes forget the power of love. We seek advice, take training classes, consult educators and professionals and try a variety of ways to become a better person and help others; when all we need is to transform, or direct, our minds toward one thing; Love. Love is a panacea for the enjoyment of life.

You want to help someone; love him or her. It doesn't matter what you are trying to accomplish by helping; using love will accomplish it. Needs comes in many forms, as well you know from interacting with people. But, no matter the need, satisfying it begins and ends with love. That's why needs can never be satisfied with sin. Sin is like being real thirsty and given a small sip of water to drink; it intensifies the thirst. You get, or obtain, but it's void of satisfaction, and saturated with selfishness; thus forcing your thinking and actions toward getting more for the same selfish reason that 's driving your thoughts. No need can be satisfied through sin. But, with love it can, because love covers all sins. That is; every need is saturated with truth, understanding, cooperation, caring and all the positives that makes life happy and successful. So, if you want to be a better person. If you want to really help others; if you really want to be an example of "God's love on this earth; then, understand the Word of God; and learn the truth about the terms modern times are using instead or love.

## Think before You Speak

Proverbs 15:28

:28 The heart of the righteous studies how to answer. But the mouth of the wicked poureth out evil things.

As you go from day to day you will encounter many situations and speak many words to nouns. You will say and do things to address what you are facing at the moment. How you react in words and actions will depend on your thinking and how well you control your emotions. Being human you are subject to all the temptations facing humanity. Therefore, in order to respond to any situation, in a positive manner, whether greeting someone or dealing with a volatile attitude, you have to think through your action, or response, before exercising it. What you do can add to, or detract from, a very bad situation. Likewise, what you do can add to, or detract from, a very loving and peaceful situation. As you deal with the facets of life think about your choice of words and what message they will convey before you speak. Just remember a hurt feeling can be just as painful as a deep gashing wound.

You can't return to yesterday; or the last second, to redo it. You can however, look at the state you're in and, if bad, change it; if good, improve it. Paul pointed up to us some of the things he had done, prior to knowing Jesus Christ. But, once he got to know Jesus, he rated everything he had done, or gained, up to that time as wasted and useless. He began, at the point of knowing Jesus, to do those things that Jesus had given him the talent and strength to do. And he became great in spreading the gospel to the gentiles, and furthering God's Word everywhere.

You; better than anyone else; know how you feel about people, places and things. You know your feelings about Jesus Christ. You know whether your actions and deeds are done in sincere love. You know your beliefs and practices. And, if you don't know whether they are in line with the Word of God, ask; God will reveal to you where the life you are living will take you. One of the greatest mistakes made by man; is thinking that by taking summation of the past, he can chart his path to the future. If you are in mire, grab hold of the hand of God and let him pull you out. (Read, understand and practice the Word of God) Don't worry about why you are in a predicament, or when you stepped in; praise God for getting you out and continue with him in obedience.

I don't know what your past is, but I do know none of us are perfect; so look at the present, see where you stand and starting this minute, look to do those things that the Bible says is good and pleases God. Your hand is on the plow, and in order to plow a straight row you have to look straight ahead. Looking back will cause you to plow a wobbly row. Treat your past deeds as Paul did; God knows them and have the power to forgive them; if you do as Paul did. Also, treat your talent as Paul did, and put it to work furthering the works of God.

## Use Your Gift To Further The Works Of God

Galatians 5:13-16

:13   For, brethren, ye have been called unto liberty; only use not liberty for an occasion to the flesh, but by love serve one another.

:14   For all the law is fulfilled in one word, even in this: thy shall love thou neighbor as thyself.

:15   But if you bite and devour one another, take heed that ye be not consumed one of another.

:16 This I say then, Walk in the Spirit, and ye shall not fulfil the lust of the flesh.

I will keep this short, because the scriptures is plain and to the point. Sisters and brothers don't use your freedom in Christ Jesus (your free will) to satisfy the lust of the flesh. There are so many wants and desires until I won't even attempt to cover them all. What I want you to think about are: don't use your gift(s) to influence others in a way that will cause them to violate God's law. It doesn't matter what your gift is; whether preacher, teacher, wisdom, knowledge, healing, discerning of spirits, interpretation of tongues, or other gifts given by God; don't use them to further a lustful cause. Example: I heard a so called minister, who had a wife, say to a married woman; it's ok for us to get together (meaning having a sexual relationship) because we are saints, and it's alright for saints to do these things. Plain and simple this liar was using his liberty in Christ to try and fulfill a lustful purpose.

If you have the ability to influence people in any way, use it to help them improve their action and reactions toward people in a way that is in line with the Word of God. Remember the old "rotten apple" moral. It only takes one bad person to spoil the group in which he associates himself. Remember also, listening to man's wisdom and disregarding God's teaching can lead you into a pit of quicksand with no help about.

God, through his son Jesus has given us freedom our minds are unable to comprehend. He loves us so much that he doesn't dictate, but let us choose our path and destination in this life; and still gives and let us enjoy the sun, rain, flowers, trees, foods, waters, air, and the list goes on. He even gives us markers along the way to let us know what road we are traveling and where we will end up on that road. He makes his commandments plain, and how to easily obey them. He shows us plainly what things are outside of his commandments; what He's please with, and what He is not please with. You have been endowed with a gift, whether you think so or not. God endowed you with love, the most powerful influencer in the world; because everyone wants and seeks it; acknowledged or not. So, if love is the only talent you have; use it to the fullest of your ability. And don't worry; it will help; not hurt. Never use anyone's trust and respect for you to further your lustful wants and desires.

## Don't Rejoice In Other's Calamity

Proverbs 24:17-20

:17   Rejoice not when thine enemy falleth, and let not thine heart be glad when he stumbleth:

:18   Lest the Lord see it and it displease Him and He turn away His wrath from him.

:19   Fret not thyself because of evil men, neither be thou envious at the wicked:

:20   For there will be no reward to the evil man; the candle of the wicked shall be put out.

Right now; think about your own children, or the person you love dearly if you don't have children. It is certain, you don't want anyone to do them bodily harm; or even think bad things about them, even if they are not all you feel they should be. You may not like their lifestyle, or some of the things they do or say, but you still love them and hope they will change. Bottom line, you love them even though you may hate things they are doing; and you will react if someone says negative things about them or do something to harm them.

God is no different when it comes to his children. And remember, all human beings are his children. God doesn't like the things many humans do, but he still loves them. And because he loves them he doesn't want anyone doing things to try and hurt them, no matter how bad their deeds are. God has a time to cut off wicked deeds and if the persons holding them refuses to let go, they will go the way of the evil deeds.

We are living in times when revenge is running rampart. People are not only seeking revenge for deeds committed against them; they are doing what they call, preventing someone from doing anything to them. The trend is; I'll get you before you get me. And, if they are successful, they rejoice greatly over it. I see it often, and I'm sure you do too, people being glad because something, other that good, happen to another person. This is, plain and simple, being envious of someone; you want to be a head higher, or one step ahead of them in everything.

## Let's Talk About Jesus

As you go about your life you are certain to see things, some bad, happening to people, or it may just be one person. If and when you see it, think about the problems or suffering that just be felled that individual, or individuals. Think about the pains and troubles it may be causing their love ones; and if all you can do is pray, ask God, with a sincere heart, to help that person, or persons. Let your feelings and actions toward those who are trying to hurt you be the same as toward those who do their very best for you. Just remember, you are not blessed by what others do to you, but by what you do to others.

## Take Note Of The Way You Worship God

Isaiah 5:20-21

:20  Woe unto them that call evil good and good evil; that put darkness for light, and light for darkness: that put bitter for sweet, and sweet fro bitter!

:21  Woe unto them that are wise in their own eyes, and prudent in their own sight!

We see in Malachi 3:6, that God do not change. God deals with sins the same now as he did in Old Testament times. The things God identified as sin in the Old Testament are still sins today and will be tomorrow. So, taking a look at verses 20 and 21 we see God is warning the people of some bad habits and practices that were violating his

Commandments. The people were bringing upon themselves, the punishment exacted by God for those deeds. God didn't just set the punishment after the sin was committed; the punishment was set from the beginning and man has always been warned of the punishments long before he committed sin.

Look at some modern day thinking and practices of trying to rationalize or make excuses for acts that violate the Word of God. I cringe, each time I hear the words "Politically correct" because I know someone is trying to make an excuse for something Godly that modern society is trying to modify. Things described by God as abominations are being modified by "Politically correct" to appear normal, good and acceptable. It doesn't matter what name we used to try and make darkness something other than what it is; darkness will remain darkness. Light will remain light; evil will remain evil, and a lie will remain a lie no matter what word or phrase is used to replace it. And, violating God's law will bring the same punishment today as it did in Old Testament times. That's why God let us have the Old Testament, so we can look back and see the mistakes of others and the punishment it brought. We can see the obedience of others and the blessing/rewards it brought. We, today, have living proof of God's love for his people and how not to bring the punishments of sins upon us.

The Old Testament is our teacher. It is our opportunity to learn by example. Think a minute about teaching your own children. You endeavor to instill in them things that will prevent them from falling into the hands of the legal system because they broke the law. You show them the trouble just one incident can get them into. How they can destroy their life with just one act that they may consider small. You teach them how not to break the law and get in trouble. In short you teach that child how to be a law abiding citizen. You do it because you love that child and want the best for him or her. God is doing the same thing for his children. God loves his children and want the best for them. He teaches his children how to be obedient to the spiritual laws governing them. God don't want to see us in trouble, bringing upon ourselves the punishment he has set for sins. God wants his children to enjoy the best; the things he prepared for us to enjoy. And, we can only do that by being obedient to his commandments.

It must be remembered: politics doesn't change the Word of God. The Word of God change politics.

## Bearing Fruit In God

John 15:7-8

:7 If you abide in Me and My Words abides in you, you will ask what you will and it shall be done unto you.
:8  Herein is my Father glorified, that ye bear much fruit; so shall ye by my disciples.

Think about this: there are rules, laws and instructions governing every aspect of our lives in society. From the moment we are born we become subject to controls. Society has laws ranging from how much water should be used to flush our toilets to what it terms: "safe amounts" of pollutions in the air we breathe, water we drink and foods we eat. And, to break the vast majority of these laws, mean suffering the punishment established for violators. So, what happen? Well, the vast majority obeys the laws without question and feels it's good to do so. By so doing the obedient ones reap the benefits of the law and are called good citizens and an asset to the community.

Well, what about the laws of God? God's laws supersedes man's laws, just as the constitution supersedes states laws. So, in order to receive the benefits of God's laws, we have to be obedient to them. And, you can be obedient to God's laws without violating man's laws just as you can be obedient to state laws without violation the constitution. However, man laws must be in accordance with God's laws just as state laws are in accordance with the constitution. The great difference is; by obeying God's laws, man is able to develop laws that are beneficial, effective, and productive in helping perform the responsibilities God left for man to carry out; love one another, help the poor, widows, homeless, and the like, and raise up children according to God's Word. By abiding in God's Word, man is able to see and feel the goodness, beauty and the effectiveness of the power of God. Jesus is saying if you obey my Words; I will give you the things you ask me for. Why, because God Word produces good things in people's lives; in other words, produces fruit. God want His every Word to bear fruit in our lives. It's the same as you plant a fruit tree or vine expecting it to bear fruit. But, what if it doesn't? You'll probably not tolerate it very long; and, get rid of it. Certainly you will not go around bragging on it; while it takes up space; use up your fertilizer, and stay fruitless.

Jesus wants us to obey his Words, because God delight in our obedience. It is a sweet aroma in his nostrils and beauty in his eyes. Think of having a child that you can delight in because he or she is obedient, law abiding, spiritual, and an all around good child. Then think of one that is just the opposite. Yes, you love them both, but which is the joy of your life and which is the sadness of you heart? We are God's children he loves us regardless, but he is not going to tell the bad ones they are good, nor the good ones they are bad. Punishments and rewards have been established. God shows us both and let us choose. He delights in good and frown at bad. You and you alone, decide whether you want to please or displease Him. By reading, understanding and following the dictates of the bible you will be fruitful and a person God glory in.

## Be Guided By God

Isaiah 55:8-9

:8  For my thoughts are not your thoughts, neither are your ways my ways, saith the Lord.
:9  For as the heavens are higher than the earth, so are my ways higher than your ways, and my thoughts than your thoughts.

Listen to what God is saying to us here. As always, let me say up front that the Word of God is meant to guide our thinking and actions in our interaction with people, places and things.

Looking at the Word we see that God is telling us to learn his Word, let it become a part of our thought process; formulating our action as we seek to earn daily bread. You have to make decisions every day of your life. From the time you wake up in the morning to the time you lie down at night you are faced with events and occurrences that you have to make a decision on. God is saying He wants us to let the Word He has given, guide us in making these decisions. It's so easy to think that we know what is best for our lives. It is easy to believe that we are doing the right thing when we act on a situation; but it's just as easy to be wrong about the whole thing. It's like a young child thinking playing in a busy street is ok. God knows the results of our actions before we do them and our thinking before the thought is formulated. So, He is telling us if we follow His teachings the results of our actions will always be good for us.

Remember, just as the sun, moon, earth and other heavenly bodies have fixed orbits; and just as something bad would happen to those bodies if they strayed from their orbits, we have a fixed path to follow; and when we stray from our fixed path nothing good will come of it. We can't think for God or act on behalf of God through our own efforts. We must rely on what God has provided; believe it; trust and use it.

If the heavenly bodies strayed from their orbits they would be all over the place; clashing into each other, causing catastrophic damage. We, clashes with one another; creating the problems we now face, because we stray from our orbit; the Word of God.

## The Blessings Of The Lord

Proverbs 10:22

:22 The blessings of the Lord, it maketh rich, and he addeth no sorrow with it.

Look at what God is saying to his people (remember we are all God's children; some are obedient and some are not). The blessings of the Lord make one rich. God Word has no boundaries so when God says His blessings will make you rich it is not limited to becoming rich in spiritual strength; it includes every need you have; money, clothing's, housing, transportation, business success, happy marriage, happy family, obedient children and much more. Every thing that is needed to enjoy the peace and happiness God give us was created from the foundation of the earth and the way to achieve it was plainly laid out by God when he created it. God didn't give us something then turn around and hide the pathway to it. He gave us both, the blessings and the way to achieve them. Now, look at the second part of the scripture; and he adds no sorrow with it. Blessings without troubles, trials, tribulations or any of the negatives that goes with man developed ways of achieving riches; that is cheating, stealing, killing, lying, destroying individuals and families, being ruthless and unkind and many more negative actions. God is saying and time has proven; that following his teaching; making it a part of everyday interaction with people, places and things will bring riches along with peace and serenity. God has taken the plotting and scheming out of becoming rich, living in peace and enjoying life; because he knows plots and schemes will never achieve riches and peace, that's why he gave us the perfect way to achieve it. Plots and schemes have three huge negatives; selfishness, greed and superiority thinking. The plotter, or schemer, always seek to achieve a selfish motive, with the thought of being smarter, stronger, bigger and to gain money, and power. This in itself shows plainly that this method is studded with sorrow, both on self and others. Because, whether acknowledged or not the schemer, or plotter, never gains peace of mind, or serenity or spirit. He or she is never at rest or at peace; and this restlessness or lack of self peace is always caste at others during daily interactions.

How often do we hear the words "I, or we, are seeking peace with this or that nation, or person?" I can safeguard you better than he or she can. Of course there are many more such sayings. These are the words of men who have no more control over the person they are referring to than a very weak stream destroying a very strong dam. These are the same lies Eve were told and believed in the Garden of Eden. Why would anyone believe that a person walking in ways, developed by man, can achieve something that comes only by following God's instructions? Guns, armies, and the weapons of war never achieved peace. It comes when individuals and nations decided within themselves that they are going to stop fighting each other and live in harmony.

That, whether acknowledged or not, is the Word of God. Violence, no matter the rationale, or in what form; war being among the reason; will never achieve peace and unity. Yes, a person or nation can be overpowered and held down for a while but the cause that started the fight in the first place is brewing inside the one overpowered and will soon erupt in the same fight all over again; making victory and peace only real in the mind of the one that saying it. God's teaching is the only way to peace and riches. Remember one thing, riches has to be complete to be riches; otherwise it's just a hand full of fools gold. Having millions, billions or trillions of man made currency does not make one rich. Riches are riches only when all concerned are affected in a positive way.

Hatred, wars, violence in any form; separation and other divisional methods, are not in God's blessing, nor did God provide a way to these things. These things come as a result of ignoring God's teaching. And anyone saying they use God's word to guide their thought and decisions each day and uses these things to accomplish a purpose, whether for self, or a nation, is clearly a liar and does not understand or practice the way of God.

If an individual or nation is blessed by God that blessing will not bring sorrow in any form to the individual, nation, or the ones that individual or nation interact with. That blessed individual or nation will not, in any form, bring sorrow, hardship, or suffering upon anyone by its decisions and actions.

As long as a person say 'I am seeking peace and understanding with others" and using other than God's

119

teachings to achieve it; that person is either lying or really don't know about God. Every need for happiness and peace was created from the foundation of the world. But, it can only be reached through following the path laid out by God.

## Believe And Trust In The Word

Matthew 5:18

:18   For verily I say unto you, till heaven and earth pass, one jot or one tittle shall in no wise pass from the law, till all be fulfilled.

When we read the New Testament it becomes clear that promises and prophecies, made in the Old Testament were all fulfilled. Now, that tells me that the promises and prophecies made in the New Testament will also be fulfilled. Many have been and the ones yet remaining will, without a doubt in my mind, be fulfilled.

The point I'm making is; whatever Jesus said he would do for you he will bring it to pass in your life time. Whatever he said you can do he will make it happen if you follow the instruction he gave. Example: St John 15:7 if ye abide in Me and My Words abide in you, ye shall ask what ye will and it shall be done unto you. So, plainly Jesus is saying if you live according to My Words you can ask for the things you both need and desire. Understand now, living in the Word removes lust and the full gambit of sins from your life.

And I will add here, the only sin you will commit is the one you don't know about, and Jesus blood covers that. So, in reality, you are living your life as laid out by Jesus Christ. And when you do, Jesus will manifest his promises in your life.

You can trust and depend on Jesus to bring his promises to pass in your life time. You ask for something and Jesus will give it to you. But remember, you have to do what he says first. This is not a "you give it to me first Jesus and then I will do what you say." You do it first, and then Jesus will act. And whether you realize it or not he is already giving you life and the goods thereof. So that and that alone, is plenty to be thankful for.

For a moment remember your past and think about this: "What would I do to someone that treats me like I've treated Jesus? What would I do or think of someone that I had given and continue to give my best to and they turned around and act like I don't even exist, much less thank me? Think about those things as you go about your daily functions.

Jesus will keep his promises to you; that you can depend on. Are you doing what he tells you to do? If not, now is a good time to start. Believe me it will pay off.

Joseph Haugabrook

Believe What God Says

Hebrews 3:15-19

:15  While it is said; Today, if you will hear His voice, harden not your hearts, as in the provocation.

:16  For some, when they had heard, did provoke: howbeit not all that came out of Egypt by Moses.

:17 But with whom was he grieved forty years? Was it not with them that had sinned, whose carcases fell in the wilderness?

:18 And to whom sware he that they should not enter into his rest, but them that believed not?

:19  So we see that they could not enter in because of unbelief.

First, read verses7-11 to see what was spoken by the Holy Spirit. And, pay close attention to what is being made plain to us, in order that we might conduct our daily affairs in a manner pleasing to God.

We talked earlier about the Old Testament and what it means to us in present times. And, we will continue to do so because we must never lose sight of the examples given by God so that we will not be tripped up by Satan's trickery, and suffer the outcome shown by the examples in the Old Testament.

In this example; all the children of Israel had to do to

own land flowing with milk and honey, was to cross the Jordan River and possess or dwell in it. But, as you know they let the report of a very, very view, sway them from believing what God had promised them. So, they rebelled, or disobeyed God. And even though they had seen the miracles wrought by God on their behalf, they let fear override reality. That is, they didn't believe God, which is the same thing as calling God a liar. And, because of their acts God said they would not enter into his rest.

Think about this; if I tell you your word is not true, I am calling you a liar. I don't care how I dress it up, the end result is; I don't believe you because I think what you are saying or have said about a thing or event will not occur; which in reality, I'm calling you a lie. Look at this: The land is yours, go possess it." No, no, God, you are sending us into a land of giants, who will surely kill us the minute we set foot on their land. In essence that was their conversation with God. Sound familiar? You read the Word, and see how simple it is to believe; and the first thing you do is say; Oh no, there has to be more to it than that. I have to do this, I have to do that, I have to look like this; I have to look like that. Thing is, you have to be obedient to what God says and no more. But, let's not stray too far a field.

Looking at the scriptures above; what is it telling us to do in our interaction with people, places and things?

Like Moses led the children out of bondage in Egypt; Jesus led us out of bondage under sin. Moses demonstrated the power and love of God to the children of Israel while leading them out of Egypt as well as in the wilderness. Yet, seeing and knowing all this, they found reasons to rebel

123

against and mistrust God. But again, all these events are examples for us today. We look at these examples and know with certainty how God views our actions. Jesus rescued us from the bondage of sin. We see again and again the power and love of God. We know His Word is true and faithful. We know, through examples, even occurrences in our own lives, that God Word will accomplish what he said it will. So, we are not to disbelieve His Word; we are to rely on it; depend on it as we fulfill our daily duties in earning our daily bread. We have to work, talk with people, help people, and interact with people in some way each day. So, while doing it let love and truth be the motivating factors for your actions and reactions. You want something, you need something; you want to help, you need to help; every day, your existence requires that you formulate and respond to ideas. Let it all be in accordance with the teaching of God. Jesus living on earth as a man demonstrated God's love and power. He gave us clear cut instructions for living. The children of Israel possessing the land, is our clear cut example of possessing all that Jesus have in store for us. But, we must believe His Word.

Do your part; God's part is already done. It's like having a safe deposit box with a bank which requires two keys. The bank representative puts his or her key in the first lock and unlocks it before you can unlock your lock. God have already unlocked his lock to your blessings and eternal life. But you must follow the rules in order to unlock your lock and receive God's promises.

Look at the example; be unbelieving, disobedient and mistrusting and you forfeit what God has already said is yours. There's no use talking about eternal life if you refuse to do what God tells you to do to gain what he has given you in this life.


## Believe

John 3:16

:16   For God so loved the world that he gave his only begotten Son, that whosoever believeth in him should not perish but have everlasting life.

Concentrate on "Believe." Somewhere along the way, in our teaching and understanding the real meaning of believe has been lost or warped beyond recognition.

Jesus is saying that whoever believes in him will not perish and will have everlasting life. Jesus warns that whatever we set our mind on doing while we are in this mortal body that is what we become. Paul, in Romans says we become a slave to these perishable things. Once our whole heart and mind become set on a thing, no matter what it is, that thing become the defining characteristic of our thinking and actions; and defines us. If it's a perishable object, defined by the Word of God as sin, then you or I become everything that perishable thing stands for; and we will perish right along with it. If our hearts are set on things that will last forever, then we become one that will last forever. Jesus tells us, and he outlines the things that are of the Kingdom of God; as well as those that are not. Now, the things that are not a part of the Kingdom of God will be destroyed, or perish. And the things of the Kingdom of God will be everlasting. If you decide to remain in a burning house, knowing it's going to be destroyed by fire, you can't expect the flames to skip over you just because you are you. You have become a part of the material fueling the fire and will go the way of the material. God let us know, the beast; Satan; and his followers will go the way prepared for them. So don't expect to worship the beast and be saved by God. Don't expect to eat candy and not get sugar in your body. Don't expect to practice what God say is wrong and expect Him to change it just because you are you.

So, what does belief have to do with all this? Well, Jesus is saying that every person that believes in him will have eternal life. So, take a close look at believing. Believing means; you fully trust, without a doubt, to the point of obeying fully the rules, regulations, guidelines, commandments or any written or spoken word by the person or persons your object of belief is directed at. With Jesus, those that trust his Words to the point of incorporating them into their everyday life will become a part of the kingdom of God and will never be destroyed; because Jesus said his Word will not pass away. Incorporating love into everything you do, being kind, caring, understanding, and doing your best, and wanting the best for others is believing in Jesus, because you are trusting his Word enough to do everything his way.

Again, believing in Jesus puts us in a frame of mind that prevent us from getting caught up in trends, popular sayings, popular practices that are invented and perpetuated by man. If the bible addresses it as wrong and sinful; it's wrong and sinful. If the bible addresses it as good and righteous; it's good and righteous; end of story.


## Be Faithful In All Your Dealings

Third John 1:2-7

:2  Beloved, I wish above all things that you mayest prosper and be in health, even as thou soul prosper.

:3  For I rejoiced greatly when brethren came and testified of the truth that is in thee, even as thou walkest in the truth

:4  I have no greater joy than to hear that my children walk in truth.

:5  Beloved, thou doest faithfully whatsoever thou doest to the brethren and to strangers

:6  Which have borne witness of thy charity before the church. Whom if thou bring forward on their journey after a Godly sort, thou shalt do well:

:7  Because that for his name's sake they went forth, taking nothing from the Gentiles.

Dealing with people, places and things starts at an early age. I'm sure you can remember when, as a small child, you had playmates you dealt with on a regular basis. And the base grew wider as you aged, and it will continue as long as you are on this earth. As you see on television, read in newspapers and hear on radios, dealings between people are not always open and above board. It hurts to see innocent people being totally deceived by those they truly trust. Think about this lady. She worked hard because she was the family sole supporter. All of her spare money was invested in stocks of one company, because she was led to believe that the stocks were sound and a good investment for her retirement. Just before retiring the company went bust under the weight of its own lies and schemes. At retirement age, this lady found herself in the predicament of trying to find another job and hopefully make enough to continue living is a decent manner. Her hope for retirement was just a distant glimmer at best. I know similar things happened to others as well, but just for a moment put yourself in the position of the deceived. Think of the trust that has been lost in business and governmental systems and, mankind in general. Think of all the joy and peace that was taken away from this one person. Think of a body that's tired and weak from age and toiling, yet, are forced to continue, because of deception. Now, put on the shoes of the deceiver. Think of a friend, coworker, or someone much closer depending on you for something they truly needed; and you, knowing full well your scheme and lies are just to benefit from their efforts. The question then becomes; how can anyone doing such things live with themselves? Did you ever look into the eyes of a person being wronged or hurt for no reason of their own? Did you ever see the hurt on a person's face when they are ridicule, mistreated or teased because they are different in stature, looks, shape or some other physical appearance? Take note sometimes. Regardless of who you are or where you live, you are depended on by others to, at the very least, be kind in your responses to them; even someone being rude want you to be kind to them. It is good to be kind and loving, because you are judged by God on how you treat others and not how others treat you. Never forget, you have the power to be good or bad; nice or rude. There is no glory or happiness in making someone feel bad. If the abuser feels some kind of elation it's only because their own feelings of unimportance are being stroked by their own ego. To put it another way; they feel so unimportant that they want others to feel it. It's no different if you are the one dishing out rudeness.

## Living Together In Christ

John 17:21

:21 That they all may be one, as thou, Father, art in me and I in thee; that they also may be one in us that the world may believe that you sent me.

Let's get right to the point. Jesus expects all men and women to live together in love, peace and harmony. Jesus showed us plainly that He and God are one because He is in the Father and the Father is in Him. And, He pointed out to us that we must be in them and they must be in us. From this relationship will flow the types of actions and reactions that will demonstrate to the world the love, mercy and grace of our Lord and Jesus Christ.

This scripture is very clear; there is no way to be in Jesus and be tainted with sin. Why do you think Jesus cried out on the cross; "My God, My God, why has Thou forsaken me?" The instant Jesus took on the sins of mankind He was separated from The Father and that separation was what was so hurting to him. Just before that Jesus prayed asking God this: "O my Father, if it is possible, let this cup pass from me; nevertheless, not as I will, but as You will." Jesus was not asking God to remove the task of taking on the sins of men. Jesus came willingly to do that. His love for mankind, His wanting the very best for mankind was His reason for doing that. No, taking on the sins of mankind was not what He was asking God to remove. It was severing the relationship they had had from the beginning. Taking on the sins of men would separate Jesus from the Father; and even though Jesus had the promise of the Father that He would not be left in that condition, the reality of being separated just for that period of time, made Him ask if he could take on the sins of men without the separation.

When we are in the Word, we are in the Father and Son. And, the Father and Son are in us. Living in the Word causes us to interact with others in love, peace and harmony. And, when that occurs, our attitudes and personalities are such that nothing but love flows out in all of our interactions with people.

Jesus said it and I know it's true. When you live in the Word and the Word live in you, the world can see the reality of what Jesus taught while on earth and left for us to follow. For from you, love, kindness and all that make life better for others will flow from you in everything you do and say.

## Let's Talk About Jesus

Just remember, mankind can live together as one, but, it cannot be done without being obedient to the commandments of God. Remember also, sin in any form separate you from the reality of the truth; and thus the relationship of; you in the Word and the Word in you.

## Truth Will Make You Free

John 8:31-32

:31 Then said Jesus to those Jews which believed on Him. If you continue in my Word, then are ye my disciples indeed;

:32 And you shall know the truth and the truth shall make you free."

There are two important factors here. "Stay in the word," and "becoming Free." Look how Jesus explains this to us. If you are in the Word you are in truth. If you are out of the Word you are out of the truth.

The important thing to note is: Jesus is not talking about "free" as established by man. Jesus is speaking of being free from things that displease God. (Displeasing God is disobeying his Laws/commandments) Jesus is telling us how to be free, or rid ourselves of these things. And look how simple it is; abide in the Word. That is, let the Word shape your thoughts, beliefs, actions and reactions as you interact with people daily. When the Word shape what we do and how we do it; we see clearly how to respond to any situation at any time in ways pleasing to God. The Word is the microscope that let us see thing as they really are. In other words, we see truth and act on truth. We understand the actions of others and react in ways pleasing to God.

Remember God created all things that are good and perfect. That which He didn't create; like lies; he let us see plain and clear. But when we reject truth or reality and pretend that what is; isn't, then we reject the Word and are saying that the Word of God is not real. In other words we believe the same lie that Eve believed it the Garden of Eden, only in different form. The things God created are good and perfect; which means our ability to talk, see, think, smell, and all the senses that makes us react to the things around us daily; are perfect. They only become imperfect when we ignore or reject what God built in us and gave us instructions on how to use them while living on earth.

All things that God created are true. All things that Satan created are lies. In order to get rid of lies; which is an enslaving burden placed on the mind and body, let the Word of God guide all that you say and do.

Love

John 3:16-17

:16   For God so loved the world, that he gave his only begotten Son, that whosoever believeth in him should not perish, but have everlasting life.

:17   For God sent not his son into the world to condemn the world; but that the world through him might be saved.

Did you, at any time in your life, wonder what it would be like to truly love someone or have someone truly love you? If it never happened to you; it has happened to many. And truly listening to people as they speak of love, it's clear many are not clear on its meaning; not knowing fully whether they are loved or not. I ask you to look at the 16th verse and understand what it's clearly saying.

God gave his best; his most precious, as a sacrifice for our sins. Jesus is not only obedient to the Father, He gave His best, His most precious, in becoming the sacrifice for our sins. That, ladies and gentlemen, is love. By freeing us from sin we are put in a position to enjoy all the beauty and wonders God has prepared for us. We can share in His beauty forever because we are judged worthy to receive it. And it's all because God gave His son and Jesus willingly suffered and gave His life for us.

Love then; wants the very best for everyone without exception. Every good thing you want for yourself, you want for others. And you not only want it for them, you do something to insure they have it. God wanted us to share in His glory. Jesus wanted us to share in the same thing. Look what They did to insure we have the opportunity to have it.
If you are seeking love, stop where you are and look to Jesus. Read the 16th and 17th verse over and over until you get its true revelation. You are loved more than you will ever understand in this life. When you realize to the extent of your ability, how much you are loved, give it to others, without

measure, without exception.

## Why Do We Fight Among Ourselves?

James 4:1

:1 From whence come wars and fighting among you? Come they not hence, even of your lusts that war in your members?

I want to make a very simple request: read the entire fourth chapter of the book of James. If you have to read it more than once to get an understanding, do it. You will find that it will give you a thorough understanding of what is happening to people; world wide.

I am going to be brief, but, I will add this; when lusts of any kind creeps into our thinking, desires, motivations, and decision making, a confused battle line is drawn between what is right and proper and what is wrong and improper. There can never be a right reason for wanting to do harm to another. In other words, there can never be justification for harming a human being in any way. I will not be judged for what people do to me, but rather what I do to people.

Why do families fight among themselves? Why do communities and states fight among themselves? And why do nations fight each other? It's lust; whether for power, prestige, money or one of the many manufactured reasons, it all boils down to one thing; lust. I want it but I don't have it so

## Let's Talk About Jesus

I'm going to get it. I have it, it's mine and I'm not going to share it.

We can love, help and share with each other; we have the capacity to do it. There is no reason to fight among ourselves. It doesn't matter what we call ourselves, we can walk hand in hand with love flowing throughout the chain.

## Love Cover All Sins

Proverbs 10:12

:12 Hatred stirs up strife, but love covers all sins.

There are two forces at work in the lives of humanity; the powerful force of love and the weak deception of hate. No matter what you do in the program of God it all leads to one thing; love. Love, as we have explained many times, wants the very best for everyone, and works to make it happen. Look at the statement: "Love covers all sins." It was love that covered our sins at Calvary. Look at Hebrews 9:22 And almost all things are by the law purged with blood; and without shedding of blood is no remission. Love led Jesus to the cross and the shedding of his blood for our sins. The spreading of love removes the deception of hate.

Hate is a lie trying to present itself as truth. In other words, hate take figments of the imagination and try to make it seem real. The whole process of hate begins with actions

135

or reactions to a non existing fact. For example: Two individuals at the request of another person trying to show them facts, sat down and wrote down facts about themselves. They wrote what they had been taught, or learned about each other in school, the community and church. They wrote down the good things each had done in the community and home. They also wrote down the bad things they had done in the home and community. The last thing they wrote down was what they wanted for themselves and their families. I don't think I have to tell you the results of the comparison. Yes, in a way, the individual deeds were different and their approach to certain goals was different, in some cases. But, after learning the facts about each other they realized much of their home teaching and what they had learned in school and the community, and in some cases, the church were, in fact, plain lies based solely on man's preferences/desires, not biblical facts. Sometimes we forget we all need the same thing to live; water, air, food. We work to make life for self and family as comfortable as possible. And even though we may do it in different ways; we are seeking the same thing from life; the best we can possibly get. So, just because we have different talents and go after what we want in different ways; shouldn't we just accept that we are all human beings, just doing different things to make life comfortable for self and family? Focusing on that would erase the lies of one person being better than another; because it would let you focus on truth and facts that; God gave us different talents to use in earning daily bread; and we should not only use what we have to earn daily bread but to make life better for all.

It doesn't matter that these two individuals were from different races, the fact is, the deeds they committed against each other were a direct result of the lies they accepted as fact. Hate comes from loving, or accepting a lie. Regardless of what is believed or said, a lie is designed to deceive, and deception ends in strife. So we see that the Word is saying hate stirs up strife. Which is saying; if there is strife it is caused by hate. Why is this true? Because fighting, murder, stealing, fornicating, and the multitude of sins against the Word of God all comes from believing something that is not true, or refusing to believe what is true.

Love will not let you do anything that will cause harm to another person, either in this world or the world to come. You will not lead someone astray knowing it will violate the Word of God; love will prevent it because you don't want that person in danger of the judgment. Love won't let you steal what others have worked for. Or take a life knowing you can't give life. Again, love makes you refrain from hurting. It causes you to strive to do your very best for others. If you find yourself chipping away at the welfare of others; stop, and ask yourself why. I can assure you it will not be found in the God's Word. The Word of God is the only authority on love and hate. Use it to overlay your words and deeds for correctness. If you feel your actions and deeds needs amending, use love to do it. That is, let love motivate your actions and deeds.

Joseph Haugabrook

## Our Relationship With Jesus

John 15:4-5

:4 Abide in me, and I in you. As the branch cannot bear fruit of itself, except it abide in the vine; no more can ye, except ye abide in me.

:5 I am the vine, ye are the branches: He that abideth in me, and I in him, the same bringeth forth much fruit: for without me ye can do nothing.

Reading the entire 15th chapter of John with specific focus on verses four and five; shows clearly how Jesus outlines our relationship with him. There is no way any person, regardless of what he or she declares to be can live a life, obedient to God's Word, without placing themselves in this relationship with Jesus. Think about going into your yard and breaking off a branch from your grape, or some other vine or tree and watch what happens to the branch. It is sure to wither and die. Also, look at the other branches left on the vine; they will continue to bring forth fruit. All of the branches, whether at the beginning of the vine or the end of the vine, will all be fed adequately from the sap flowing in the vine. No branch will be treated differently because of its position on the vine. The vine itself takes from the soil the necessary nutrients to provide for the fruit all the ingredients to make it what it ought to be; color, taste, and all the other necessary things that make it unique. Without the vine the branches are doomed; and all will die. In order for you to be the unique person God made you, you must get what you need from Him. He is the source for you to produce the fruit you were created to produce.

Jesus wants us to understand that life itself is dependent upon his love, mercy and grace; there in no way any man on earth can give you life if Jesus cut you off. Getting the big-head, saying I can do this or that on my own; is foolish; like disregarding the truth, and facts of life. It's like saying I can jump out in front of a speeding locomotive, dare it to hit me, and it will instantly stop; yea, right!

You will notice in this chapter that all the good things of life can be had, in this life time, and that includes the riches of the world with peace of mind, love and concern for others, true happiness, a loving family, a successful career, and more; but, those things comes through recognizing the "vine branch" relationship with Jesus.

Yes, there are other ways of gaining riches, you see it around you each day, but it doesn't come with peace of mind, caring, happiness, and loving families to name a few. Ways; other than what Jesus explains here; comes with deceptions, pain, and evils thrown in by Satan; and you need no reminding of that, just look at the way people are being deceived today. Look at the way society is trying to make people in general accept lies as truth, and wrong as right.

The vine branch relationship with Jesus is important in understanding how to interact with people, places and things you encounter each day.

Joseph Haugabrook

## Don't Be Surprise At What The World Do And Say To You

John 16:1-3

:1 These things have I spoken unto you, that ye should not be offended.

:2 They shall put you out of the synagogues: Yea, the time cometh, that whosoever killeth you will think that he doeth God service.

:3 And these things will they do unto you, because they have not known the Father, nor Me.

Jesus is speaking to the disciples and his people for all times. He is telling you of actions brought against you by those who do not know Him or the Father. They will try in every way to discourage or prevent you from living a holy life; that is, being good, truthful, honest, loving, caring, concern, trustworthy and the likes. They will go so far as to kill you for living as Christ said live; and, try to justify it. One of the common ills you see or hear about is; people calling the authorities on parents, who are doing nothing more that rearing their child or children in a strict, but proper manner. Doing the right thing will not always be seen in the right light. And being truthful about a matter or situation will not always gain you friends. I told a gentleman one day, he was wrong for feeling on another man's wife in an improper way. Needless to say he became angry at me and for a long time, didn't speak. He knew he was wrong, but didn't want a mirror held up to his face so he could see himself. King Herod knew John was right when he told him he was wrong for having his brother's wife. But, he didn't want to hear the truth. Feelings and attitudes are still the same. That's why Jesus said, men love darkness rather than light. An alcoholic doesn't want to be told he's one. A husband or wife gets angry with the mate for catching him or her cheating. People in general do not want to be told they are wrong; no matter how wrong they are.

Jesus is saying because there are some that don't understand, and will not accept the truth, they will go to the extreme to cover up their deeds. So when people speak out against you for doing good, don't be discouraged, just keep doing what Jesus told you to do; love one another. The people coming against you should not be hated for their deeds, because they really and truly don't know the evil they are committing against their own soul. You should keep them in your prayers and continue your efforts to keep righteousness before them. We are living in times when evil seems to be more prevalent than good, but don't despair, good is present and is always in more abundant that evil; and certainly more powerful.

## Why?

I John 3:1

:3 Behold what manner of love the Father has bestowed upon us, that we should be called the sons of God! Therefore the world knoweth us not, because it knew him not.

141

## Joseph Haugabrook

I think it's safe to say, sometime in your life you have either asked yourself, or wondered, "Why am I going through this? Or, why is this happening to me?" Why indeed. Why do we have to face so many negatives in life; negative conversations, attitudes, morals, thinking, teachings, practices and the list goes on. Negatives produce; to name a few; greed, lust, infidelity, addictions of all sorts and much more that surrounds us each day. Why; where do they come from, and why do we all face them?

If, for example, you traveled a road each day that was well built, smooth, solid, no pot holes, bumps or anything bad about it. And, let's say, the conditions where this road is; weather, temperatures, and other climatic conditions were ideal with no negative effects on the road; such as washing rains, extreme temperatures that would degrade materials, no heavy equipment that would crash the road, In other words, you have an ideal road to travel with conditions ideal to keep it that way. So, each time you drove onto that road you wouldn't have to even think about pot holes, bumps, or flying objects thrown up by tires of other cars damaging your car. You could peacefully sail along being happy and thankful.

Well, that's the road of life God built for us; the perfect road with ideal conditions. But, if we look at Revelation 12:12, which read: "Therefore rejoice O heavens and you who dwell in them! Woe to the inhabitations of the earth and the sea! For the devil has come down to you, having great wrath, because he knows that he has a short time." Here we find the "why" for the pot holes, bumps, and wash outs in the perfect road of life God built.

# Let's Talk About Jesus

The devil, through encouraging human beings, our sisters and brothers, make the road rough and dangerous. It is through Satan's encouragement, that men and women commit the sins they do. And they do it because they have been blinded by the lies of Satan. Don't be deceived. If the devil convinced, with his lies, many angels in heaven to side with him he can convince you, unless you follow the Word of God, as written in His Holy bible. Remember what Jesus said when the devil tried his tricks on Him. "Satan, it is written." It is written is our cue to use the Word to get Satan off our backs; or, out of our thoughts, actions and reactions.

This road we travel daily and must travel is full of sins; lust, greed, hate, addictions, deception and the list goes on. And unless you use the Word of God as your guidance you are like a soldier traveling through an enemy's mine field. You know destruction is all around you and you have to be extremely careful not to be destroyed by it. Satan hates anyone and anything that love and honor Jesus Christ. One wrong step and you step on one of his mines of destruction. In other words you become blinded by his lies.

When you are treated badly or unfairly by other human beings, your sisters and brothers, you have to keep in mind it is happening to you because they have been blinded by the devil to truth and righteousness, and are doing just like the angels that sided with him did; fight against the works of God.

So, I urge you; use the Word of God to guide you around the negatives Satan places in your path. You will be tempted by lust, greed, cheating, infidelity, lying and a host of other negatives; recognize them for what they are and stick with what is written in the bible.

The world (those doing evil) does not know you. (Those doing righteousness) In other words those doing evil acts against those doing righteous acts do not understand that what they are doing is wrong. They have been deceived by Satan. That's why it is so important that you don't try to seek revenge against them. In many cases, your continual good, will win over some that will realize that what you are doing is far better than what they are doing. Remember Jesus Words on the cross: "Father forgive them, for they know not what they do."

## Don't Forget Who He Is

John 14:6-11

:6 Jesus saith unto him, I am the way, the truth and the life: no man cometh unto the Father, but by Me.

:7 If ye had known Me, ye should have known My Father also; and from henceforth ye know Him and have seen Him.

:8 Philip saith unto Him Lord, shew us the Father and it sufficeth us.

:9 Jesus saith unto him, Have I been so long time with you and yet hast thou not known Me, Philip? He that hath seen Me hath seen the Father, and how sayest thou then, shew us the Father?

:10 Believest thou not that I am in the Father, and the Father in Me? The words that I speak unto you I speak not of myself; but the Father that dwelleth in Me, He doeth the works.

:11 Believe Me that I am in the Father and the Father in Me; or else believe Me for the very works sake.

Isn't it ironic how easy it is to become so caught up in the physical things that the spiritual things slips from memory? Take another look at the statement Philip made and think about the world around you. Now keep in mind, this is not to criticize Philip, but to look at how easy it is to forget the present and power of God.

In today's society every time some one makes a statement of give advice, it has to be backed up by some physical study on the subject. It's ironic how easy it is to be branded an expert just because you go out and talk to X number of people, get their opinion on the subject, call it a study and say these are the findings. You instantly become an expert or a noted author. Think about it, just recording what others think makes you an expert; yet reading the Bible, understanding what it teaches and tell others, instantly brands you a religious zealot or a nut.

I don't have to remind you of all the studies that are going on in society today. And getting caught up in these physical efforts can make you forget who Jesus is and His spiritual present in the world.

The power of God is present in everything we see and do. Jesus told Philip, if you are having doubt, look at the works and believe them. What we have to look at, in present times, are the unchanging promises of God. One example is: the rainbow that God gave as a sign that he would not send rain again on the earth as he did when he covered it with water. Look at how long that has been and we still see a rainbow after a rain. Sure, some tries to justify why it's there, using man's rationale, but the fact is, God said it would always be and it still is. Look at the things Jesus said would take place as time progressed toward the ending of this present system of things as we know it. These events are occurring as told by Jesus and the prophets. If you still have doubt, look at the power of God that keep everything in the vast universe in perfect timing; sunrise, sunset, ever orb of the universe in it's own orbit, and the list goes on. He provides many miracles, right before our eyes each day; the miracle of birth by every living creature, to perpetuate the specie as God commanded. Still doubtful, study for a few days, the brain and nervous system, and ask yourself; could this be brought about by some haphazard system; or the universe formed by some big bang, not associated with God's power? What I'm trying to get you to see is; don't get so caught up in physical studies, and scientific theories that you forget the teachings of Jesus and lose sight of reality. I heard a judge asked a question a few weeks ago that really stunned me. A lady in court stated that she was teaching her daughter to overcome an attitude problem she had developed from associating with a group of kids that neither respected themselves nor others. Keep in mind the mother had made progress with her daughter. The judge belittled the lady by asking if she was a trained counselor, or physiologist, and how did she know she was not doing more harm than good; as if counselors could predict the future and had powers to make their efforts a guaranteed success.

## Let's Talk About Jesus

The girl was ordered into counseling as the lady's efforts were totally rejected by the judge. Counseling by parents and people of God are very seldom sought by the law enforcement arena. And, without condemning, I think that is sad because it pushes aside the wisdom and knowledge given by God to rear children in the right way.

Don't forget who Jesus is and what He can do for you in accomplishing the things you have to do each day. Remember his Words; Greater is He that is in you than he that is in the world. In other words, the power and understanding you possess when you allow Jesus to abide in you (guiding our thinking process) is far more than enough to make you victorious in all your good efforts.

## Trust In Jesus

Psalm 37:3-4

:3   Trust in the Lord, and do good; so shall thou dwell in the land and verily thou shalt be fed.

:4   Delight yourself also in the Lord, and He shall give you the desires of thine heart.

For a brief moment; pause and ask yourself: Am I looking to Jesus to have a place prepared for me after this life?

The question bears thinking about all the time because we are looking for a heavenly home when this life is over, which means we are looking for Jesus to have us a place of rest for eternity. So, with that being true, why is so little trust being put into Jesus providing our everyday needs? Look at verse 4; "Give you the desires of your heart. That covers everything a person could want in this world and the world to come. You are covering all bases; the desires of your heart on earth and a heavenly home in the next life. Now, look at verse 3; because this is where our actions come in. In order to obtain the desires of our hearts and a heavenly home later, we must follow instructions; and our first instruction is to "Trust in Jesus." One quick note: If you do not trust him for earthly needs, you are only fooling yourself to think you trust him for heavenly needs.

Again, we are looking for that eternal home; we sing about it, we pray about it, we hope for it, yet we fail to trust him for the things we need in our daily lives on this earth. Isn't that hypocritical? It's saying; I trust you for heavenly things after this life, but not for things to sustain this life on earth.

Think about this. In spring and summer seasons many, probably you among them, will head for vacations and the like. You will, trust in your car, van, motor home, air flights, trains, ocean liners, boats and whatever mode of transportation you use to get you to, from, and around during your vacation. Your trust in your plans and these objects are steadfast and sure; so much so that you go to great length making certain everything is ready to carry out your vacation plans. What it means is you are trusting man and man made objects to do what man says will be done. If you can put that kind of trust in man and see the deceptions, greed and corruption committed by him daily; can't you put that same trust in Jesus who have proven that trusting in his Word brings the things you want and need in this life; with him having proven his promise are totally fulfilled in the life to come? One more thing; trusting in Jesus assures you, man's deceptions will be revealed to you before they happen; and, He's with you no matter what comes.

## The Lord Is My Shepherd

Psalm 23:1

:1  The Lord is my shepherd: I shall not want.

The lord is my shepherd! Look at the meaning of these five words. These words have a deep meaning with far reaching effects. Remember what Jesus said; "I am the good shepherd." A good shepherd tends his flock well. He makes sure their needs are fully met. The flock doesn't have to worry about food, water, shelter, safety, and being maltreated; they are relaxed and happy in the reality that their shepherd knows and provides their need. The flock knows there are wolves wanting to destroy them. They know there are times the grass will become thin. They know that a water source might dry up. They knows that in order to travel from a thin source of food to a rich one, it might require a brief time of hunger, or a brief moment of thirst, but they don't worry because they know their good shepherd is leading them to green pastures and still waters. In other words they know they will not die of thirst or starvation, and

149

not be destroyed by the enemy along the way. They rejoice while traveling through thin times just as they do during times of plenty. Think about that over and over until it becomes a part of your daily life. Don't lose faith in the shepherd just because of a brief thin period.

Jesus is our shepherd. He knows Satan and his imps are out to destroy us. He knows we have need of food, water, shelter, clothing and safety. Jesus sees our needs every clock tick of our lives. Yes, our resources may get thin at times and it seems we may not be able to satisfy our needs. But, if you trust in your good shepherd you will soon be in green pastures again with plenty of still waters to drink from. Remember what Paul told the people on the ship when things really looked bad because of the storm. He made it plain to them that they had to stay on the ship to be spared. Had anyone jumped ship he would've perished. If you leave the flock you are subject to all the forces that want to destroy you. You wander around because you don't know where the sources of your needs are. You try things that just don't pan out, because you are being blinded by the enemy without knowing it. You are wandering without direction and eventually you will wander off a cliff into deep rapids or be eaten by the one seeking to destroy you.

Yes, trouble is all around you, bills piles up, your body and spirit seems weak; it seem your needs will never be met. But remember, you are being led by a good shepherd; a shepherd that loves you and will not see you die or starvation or thirst if you don't wander from the flock

Let's Talk About Jesus

Set Priorities In Proper Order, And God Will Heal All Problems.

Psalm 115:16 And 2 Chronicles 7:14
:Psalm 115:16  The heaven, even the heavens are the Lord's; but the earth has he given to the children of men.

:2 Chronicles 7:14  If my people which are called by my name, shall humble themselves, and pray, and seek my face, and turn from their wicked ways; then will I hear from heaven, and will forgive their sin, and will heal their land.

God's plan for mankind, as it was from the beginning, is still in place and functioning as designed by God.

Psalm 115:16 tells us all things belong to God, but he gave the earth to man to tend and care for; to live together, be loving, prosperous and enjoy the beauty that he placed in it when he created it and the changes that takes place as time  reshape many things. With time, God let the winds and waters change shapes and views, keeping them fresh and interesting; making life interesting for man. He also instilled a beautiful unchanging and interesting feature in every man; love. Love keeps life fresh, interesting, joyous and prosperous. And mankind is not to add or take away from what God assigned as permanent. I don't have to tell you, all you have to do is look around you to see the damage being done to mankind by trying to make sex love, and love sex. It has and continues to destroy generations. Man is the caretaker of this earth, and the problems covering it today is the result of mankind being a bad caretaker. The land is filled with sin, and man is looking to man instead of God to solve the problems caused by his sins.

Look at 2 Chronicles 7:14. My people; who are called by my name. Humble themselves. Pray. seek My face. Turn from their wicked ways. I will hear from heaven; forgive their sin. Heal their land.

God is saying plainly that; mankind need to set his priorities in the proper order. Example: I accept God as my Lord and Master. I get rid of the false pride, nasty attitudes, lying, cheating, false egos, adultery, envy and all the negatives that are contrary to God's Word. I remain humble in my interaction with others, which is before God. I realize that I don't have the answers, and I should seek guidance, always, from God. I should never let thoughts that violate God's Word take shape in my heart. Such thoughts should be shredded as they enter my mind. When I do this I am setting my priorities in the proper order. In other words, I realize that God ways are the answer to all my problems and I seek his guidance in all that I do. God is saying; when mankind realize that my ways are set and will not change to satisfy his whims, and return to the way I set forth, then, I will answer his pleas, forgive his sin and remove the things causing him to suffer. There is no such thing as the earth can't be a peaceful place to live. There is no such thing as man cannot live in love and harmony. It can be done, but first, man must set his priorities in order. Can't be done; is a lie straight from hell!

Think about this: if you gave your children a piece of land that had all the resources they need to live happy and prosperous. Wouldn't you want them to be appreciative enough to take care of it and keep it in a manner that would continue to support them and the grandchildren coming after them; and not let it become over run by wild weeds, and all kinds of vile destructive creatures? Well, this is what's happening to the earth God gave to mankind. The earth is being over run with every vile act and sin.

## YOUR DAILY SERVICE

Malachi 1:6-8

:6 A son honors his father, And a servant his master. If then I be a Father, where is my honor? And if I be a master, where is my fear? Saith the Lord of hosts unto you, O priests, that despise my name. And ye say, Wherein have we despised thy name?

:7 Ye offer polluted bread upon mine altar; and ye say, Wherein have we polluted thee? In that you say, The table of the Lord is contemptible.

:8 And if ye offer the blind for sacrifice, is it not evil? and if you offer the lame and sick, is it not evil? Offer it now unto thy governor; will he be pleased with thee, or accept thy person? saith the Lord of hosts.

We've mentioned this in previous subjects but it bears visiting again. You see, the spirit of selfishness, which are causing many problems in families, communities, and nations, abound in these present times. This is not to say you have succumb to selfishness, it is to say that it is around you and you should check your attitudes, ego, actions and reactions to make sure it has not crept in unaware. It's like checking your car for the things that keeps it running good, and staying safe. You make sure your tires are not damaged, or worn to prevent blowouts and possibly harming you and others. You make sure the oil is adequate, to prevent engine damage, and so on. Selfishness is a hazard that, if not noticed, will creep in and cause a tragedy in your daily interaction with people.

Let me emphasize here; your daily interaction with people; that is, what you do, how you do it; what you say, how you say it. Your feelings and attitudes toward people are your offerings to God. It's what you are offering to God daily. God knows, but you must ask yourself; am I making an unblemished offering to God or is it polluted with hate, lust, adultery, addictions, disobedient, or some other thing that Cod says is not of his kingdom?

Remember too; it is not what you do in a congregation, whether weekly or some other frequency that matters to God; it is what you do all the time, every living minute of your life. Remember God's Word, he that endureth to the end shall be saved. That means being obedient to His Word all the way.

Look at the scriptures above; think about what it is saying. You are offering something that God has plainly said not to offer. In other words, you are treating people, everyone you interact with daily, in ways God said not to treat them.

When you rationalize that treating other in a nasty or evil way is right; you are saying God's way is not the right way and you have to correct it.

Think of this one example; you are a cashier in a store, a customer comes through your line to be checked out and for some personal reason whether bad hair day, hate for a group, don't want to work, or some other reason; you are unkind, or down right nasty. You do this and feel the customer have to, or should, accept it. Would you do that to the owner, or someone you thought the owner respected or loved? Remember now, the customers are responsible for your paycheck.

Well, God is responsible for your life, health and strength. Believe it or not, every good thing in your life comes from God. God does not give you evil things; whatever evil comes into your life you reach out and grab it against God's will.
We don't; in present times, offer animals, doves, and the like, for sacrifice. Our offerings are our treatments of God's creations. Your actions and reactions, whether physically, mentally, in prayer or deeds, are your offering to Jesus Christ. He is our God, our Savior, the giver of the good things we have and love. Doesn't he deserve to be offered your best? Especially since your best only brings good into your life.

If we look closely at today's practices, things of Malachi's times parallel today's practices. Look at two of the many vital lessons in the 6th verse: The Father/son; servant/master, and, the priest/people/God relationship. First,

God asks the question; "If you say you are my son or servant; then, why are you not acting like a son or servant? A son, God said, honors his father and a servant his master. So, why are you not acting like what you say you are? (Hold that thought for a moment)

Second: God speaks expressly to the priest. God is telling the priest; 'You despise my name." The priest asks, "What have we done for you to say we despise your name?" God answer them this way. Your offering should be without blemish. Yet you offer the blind, sick and lame; is this not ignoring my commandment to you. Is this not evil? Is this not saying you are my son or servant and ignoring what I've told you to do. Try this on your governors (kings, and the like; those that rules over you) will they accept such disobedience? Take them a sick cow or lamb to eat; you think they will pat you on the back for it?

Now, look closely at what the people of God were doing, including the priest and what is happening in our present times. The priests were offering on God's Altar what the people brought to them for offerings. And the people were bringing what they considered no good or not of much value. It's the same as a super rich man giving a poor man a pair of shoes that he was about to throw away because of holes in the soles; and a leader who witnessed the act praised the rich man for being so generous. In short, the people were breaking the commandments of God and the priest were a party to the disobedience. The priest knew, just as the people knew, that their offering violated the commandments of God, yet they both continued with their disobedient acts and practices.

Let's Talk About Jesus

In present times, the acts and deeds of the people and ministers parallel those of Malachi's time. I don't have to tell you that many sermons preached every Sunday morning are formatted in a way to please the wishes of the congregations. Pastors and ministers are hired by the congregation and are making their sermons fit the acts and deeds of the congregation. People should come to church with love, understanding, cooperation, sharing, caring, positive attitudes and all the positives found in the Word of God. This is what they should bring to the minister and congregation. The priest, using the Word of God should show them how to be even more loving and positive. This is bringing unblemished, or the best offerings to God.

Look at the people during Malachi's time; they didn't intentionally raise lame, sick, blind livestock, but it happened in the herds. And, falling prey to evil thoughts, they began an evil practice of using these animals for offerings. People today may not intentionally set out to be evil or do evil, but it happen in their life and they let these happenings turn into an evil practice. They harbor hate in their hearts. They become selfish, filled with greed, lust, become addicted and worse. And accepted or not, this is what they live each day, what they use in their interaction with people, and take to church on Sundays. And, since the pastor happens to be a hireling he or she will bow to the wishes of the congregation in order to keep their job. If we look at leaders, whether in the pulpit, communities, or higher, we find them doing the will of those that put them in the position; leaving the true gospel out of the picture. God's name may be used, but not in the manner God prescribed.
So, are polluted offering being made today? Yes, and a

thousand times yes; polluted offerings are being made to God. Jesus taught us how to make acceptable offerings to God; did we forget? Have we pushed his teachings aside? Who's that in the pulpit? Who's that on the deacon board/board of elders? Who's that in the elected offices? Who are these leaders? Look closely, then look in the mirror and ask; who am I?

## WE NEVER KNOW WHO GOD IS USING OR WHY

Romans 9:10-18

:10 And not only this: but when Rebecca also had conceived by one, even by our father Isaac;

:11 (For the children being not yet born, neither having done any good or evil, that the purpose of God according to election might stand, not of works, but of him that calleth:)

:12 It was said unto her, The elder shall serve the younger.

:13 As it is written, Jacob have I loved, but Esau have I hated.

:14 What shall we say then? Is there unrighteousness with God? God forbid.

:15 For he saith to Moses, I will have mercy on whom I will have mercy, and I will have compassion on whom I will have compassion.

:16 So then it is not of him that willeth, nor of him that runneth, but of God that showeth mercy.

:17 For the scripture saith unto Pharaoh, even for this same purpose have I raised thee up, that I might show my power in thee, and that my name might be declared throughout all the earth.

:18 Therefore hath he mercy on whom he will have mercy, and whom he will he hardeneth.

This is a very powerful message to God's children. Think about what it is saying. Look at Esau and Pharaoh, and then think about the professions and conditions existing in the world today. I'm not going to try and list everything, for it would take many volumes to do so. But, what Jesus wants us to know is very plain. We are not to judge people one way or the other. Our function in life is to love, understand, be cooperative, help in any way we can, and always keep unrighteousness out of our thinking, actions and reactions. Whatever we see someone doing or saying, our duty is to avoid judging him or her, but rather giving all the love and help we can. That help comes from constant prayer and fasting, asking Jesus to direct all of our actions and reactions. Not from some spur of the moment holier than thou attitude.

Let God work his perfect works in humanity. He knows who he is using and why. Who knows; you may need the very thing you are judging, to make you a better person. Jesus never said our works would make us free. He said "the truth" will make us free. Therefore it is not how we perceive

159

things to be that make them a reality, it's how God says things are that makes them reality.

We have to keep one thing in mind as we live this life. No one made themselves, and no individual made another, it was God that did the making. Therefore it is God that determines whether the action of each individual is of Him or Satan. God, not man or woman, is the only one that can judge righteous judgment. Beside, what benefit can be derived from judging another, except a vain sense of self worth, which is the same as holier than thou.

Read the 9th chapter of Romans over and over until the Spiritual, not book meaning, is seared in your heart and mind.

## GOD HEARS US NO MATTER WHAT PREDICAMENT WE ARE IN

Jonah 2:1-2

:1 Then Jonah prayed to the Lord his God from the fish's belly

:2 And he said: I cried by reason of mine affliction unto the Lord and he heard me; out of the belly of hell cried I, and thou heardest my voice.

You know the story of Jonah; how he came to be in

the belly of the fish. It is a great example of one man not wanting to be obedient and do what God had told him to do. So, what did he do? He followed his own mind and ended up in deep, life threatening trouble.

This great example demonstrate to us today how easy it is to get in trouble following our own mind and doing our own thing rather that what Jesus tells us to do. We put ourselves in life threatening positions by ignoring what Jesus tells us, in His Holy Word, to do. We see through Jonah's mistakes that nothing good comes from disobeying what God has so plainly laid out for us to do. Jonah brought all his problems on himself. But in spite of his disobedience God still heard his prayer and delivered him out of his predicament. That is a great lesson for us today. We get ourselves in some tight spots because of our own actions. But we have hope, if we realize as Jonah did, that we have done something to get us in whatever predicament we find ourselves, and pray to Jesus to forgive our error and return to obedience.

One of the great things about this example is; it is open ended. Meaning, it will fit whatever problem you are having right now and it will continue on into eternity. I don't know what your problems are now or will be in the future, but, if you find yourself in trouble, whether with family, friends, on the job, with the law, or whatever, call on Jesus Christ for deliverance. Don't try to figure out what you did wrong just be sincere in your desire and effort to rid yourself of your problems through being obedient to the commands of Jesus Christ.

There was no way Jonah could have controlled that

fish from the inside of his belly. In other words Jonah had no control of the situation, but, he knew God did and he prayed to God, who could control the situation and through prayer he received the help needed to get him out of trouble.

Because of the thinking and practices of people today it is very easy to believe that we can do things our way. Teen pregnancy rages because teens feel they can do things their way. Violence rages because people decide to do things their way. Addictions of all kinds rage because people decide to do things their way. The bad and evil acts are occurring because many don't realize that there are consequences for their actions. And, like Jonah, they find too late their acts have gotten them into a deep mess. It's easy to see that many don't do what Jonah did; turn to God for deliverance; they turn to more of the same or to other to abet them in their wrong doing. And it reaches from the homeless to the Whitehouse. Jesus sees us at all times and knows what we get ourselves into. He will help us if we pray sincerely to be delivered. Have a problem? Turn to Jesus the one that can control the situation. Jesus loves you and will take case of you. This help was not unique to Jonah; it is for all of us for all times. But, you have to do what Jonah did. He prayed for help because he had learned his lesson and was not going to be disobedient again; but continue in obedient. You can't just pray to be delivered from the problem you are in and then return to disobedient. You have to be sincere in continuing to being obedient to God's Word. Just know you can't scam God.

## POWERFUL COMMANDMENTS OF GOD

Genesis 2:17 And John 13:34

Genesis 2:17   But of the tree of the knowledge of good and evil you shall not eat of it; for in the day that thou eatest thereof thou shalt surely die.

John 13:34 A new commandment I give to you, that you love one another; as I have loved you, that you also love one another.

You've probably heard how simple things were for Adam in the Garden of Eden; just one commandment to obey. God pointed out the tree and told Adam why he should not eat the fruit from it. There were nothing else to worry about; no sin or evil, and to keep it that way all Adam had to do was obey the one thing God told him to do.

In present times, God did not heap a lot of commandments on us. Just like in the days of Adam, he gave us only one. Why? Jesus suffering and death cleared our slate of sin. His blood restored things as it were in the days of Adam before sin.

Jesus commanded us to love one another in the same manner that he loved us. If that one commandment is followed, it will eliminate every sin being committed by man. If that commandment had been followed, by men, when Jesus purged sin from among men through his blood, then man's relationship with God would have returned to the days of Adam, prior to his disobedient act. But, like Adam, men

163

disobeyed the commandment to love. Just like Adam did with forbidden fruit. Disobedient to God's word equals sin. It's no different now than it was with Adam.

Today, we have one commandment to obey; Love. If we love everybody the same way Jesus loved us, it will incorporate all the things Jesus tells us to make a part of our lives. Stop trying to itemize sin, and worry if you are sinning or not, just concentrate on love. Think, live and respond in love. Let your whole being become love; that is: wanting the best for others and working to make it happen. You'll note in the Old Testament, God gave the children of Israel the Ten Commandments which incorporated all things the Israelites were to do, or not do. The Ten Commandments spelled out sin so there would be no mistake. In other words, the Israelites couldn't use not knowing what sin was as an excuse. This again was necessary, because through Adam's disobedience sin had entered the world and needed defining.

We find, in the New Testament, many things that we should and should not do, but they are all embodied in the commandment of "love one another." Love itself sets up do's and don't. Love is a fine filter that let good flows through and keeps evil out. And, just like in the Old Testament, these things are necessary because man disobeyed the commandment to love one another. Your mind is constantly bombarded with good and bad, and you need something to separate the two. Jesus gave us that separator; love.

One commandment in the Old Testament: Don't eat of the fruit.

One commandment in the New Testament: Love one another.

If you just concentrate on loving everybody, without exception everything else will fall in place. If you want to serve God in the fullest, be obedient to his commandment to love.

Love is the only eraser of sin. You love Jesus, by being obedient to his words. You serve him by loving others in the same manner he loved us all.

## WORDS AND ACTIONS WITHOUT LOVE

I Corinthians 13:1

:1 Though I speak with the tongues of men and of angels, and have not charity, I am become as sounding brass, or a tinkling cymbal.

There are two great truths in this scripture;
(A) no matter what we do in this life, if it's not done in love it is nothing; spiritually.
(B) We don't see the big picture. Putting it another way, we don't see God's entire program for man at any one time in this life. We only see it in parts; therefore we only understand in part; that's why faith is so necessary.

Look at what the scripture is saying. All the things God told the prophets to do; the things Jesus told his disciples to do; all are completely filled with love. We know the meaning of love is: wanting the very best for others and doing all you can to make it happen; so, the point God is hammering home is: let your thoughts and deeds be formulated and carried out in love. If it's done without love it is nothing but wasted effort in his sight. In other words, it does nothing to further the programs of God. It's like making your favorite sweets and leaving out the sweetener. It doesn't matter that you put in all the other ingredients, if the sweetener is left out, your favorite sweet become blah, and your efforts will have been in vain. In order for God's program to turn out as he has planned, all ingredients must be present. We, all people, are the cooks; our deeds are the ingredients, and God wants us to know what He is allowing to be put in because His program is going to be what He said it would be, and do what He said it will do. Therefore the ingredients we put in must be what God said would be allowed; He will not allow anything else in. If we try, it will just be wasted effort on our part. That's why Jesus said in Matthew 7:23, and then will I profess unto them I never knew you; depart from me, ye that work iniquity. There is an old saying; "don't be fooled by imitation, get the real McCoy. Learn, understand, and put into God's program what He has ordained. Be kind, loving, caring, understanding, cooperative, peaceful, and sharing in everything you do and say to all people every day.

Just remember, God is showing us here, plain and simple, that Love is the most important ingredient in His program, and every word or deed inserted by us must be filled with love.

Let's Talk About Jesus

## MAKE SURE OTHERS SEE THE LIGHT IN YOU

Matthew 5:14-16

:14 You are the light of the world. A city that is set on a hill can not be hidden

:15 Nor do men light a candle, and put it under a bushel, but on a candlestick; and it giveth light unto all that are in the house.
:16 Let your light so shine before men that they may see your good works and glorify your Father which is in heaven.

Every one on earth will, in some way, affect the life of one or more people as they go through life and are therefore, in their own right, a teacher or example for someone.

The summary of the lesson Jesus is teaching us here is: Our deeds; actions, reactions, responses and interactions with others, are the way they see us. Our deeds will determine whether they believe and trust what we are saying to them. When it comes to interacting with others; words means nothing unless those words match the attitudes and dispositions being displayed.

Jesus is showing us here that it is imperative that we practice His teachings and let it dictate and control our actions at all times whether we are interacting with people, places and things, or resting on our beds in thought. It's possible to have a good attitude toward people in their present, but harbor evil thought behind their backs. It is also possible, and does happen, to talk a good game without

167

obeying the rules. It is easy to tell someone else to do something without you following what you are asking others to do. It's not hard to find people that are very knowledgeable of God's Word but, their deeds are not matching the words they speak. Jesus want you to understand that once you read and understand his Words there are thing you must do with that wisdom and understanding.

1) Don't keep it to yourself; that is: put it under a bushel.

2) Let it control your thinking, actions and reactions; letting it shine before men that they may see your good work; your good deeds; and glorify your Father in heaven. (Many will see how your good deeds are helping others and start doing the same thing themselves.)

This is all about living your life daily among the people of the world; in your home, your community, at work, shopping, relaxing, on vacation or the other hundred of things you do while earning daily bread and on your personal time.

There is a saying: "Talk is cheap." It holds true here. It's not talk that demonstrates to people how good God is in your life; it's your attitude; the way you respond to both easy and difficult problems life poses. It's easy to tell someone not to get upset over something: but, what happen when you are faced with the same or worse condition? Are you calm or do you become frustrated? Remember what you do is seen by someone, at some time; and things always have a way of going full circle. So, becoming frustrated over something you teach others to be calm about will, in time, get back to the one you gave advice to. That is why Jesus wants us to always use his Word in teaching others about life. No matter what you say, if it is in accordance with the Word of God it will always hold true and remain the same.

Again, let us remember the Word of God is about our lives on this earth. The deeds we do in this life are either in accordance with God's Word; and thereby earn us eternal life with Him; or, they are not in accordance with His Word; thereby earning us the damnation that goes with disobedience.

## WHY MEN SIN SO EASILY

Matthew 10:28
:28 And fear not them which kill the body, but are not able to kill the soul: but rather fear him which is able to destroy both soul and body in hell.

To fear is also to respect. We don't grab hold of a high power electric line because we know what the electric power in the line will do to our body. So we have fear of its destruction and respect for it destructive power. This fear or respect prevents us from being harmed by keeping away from the power line.

Let me ask you: how many criminals do you know will perform their offense with policemen all around them? You think a rapist will perform his sadistic act with a policeman standing near him? Will a bank robber ignore law enforcement agents filling the bank and commit his act? The fact is; criminals commit their acts because they believe they will not be seen by the police and will therefore get away with it. Unless men are bent on self destruction, they do not do things that will lead to it.

Where sins and evils of all sorts are present there is no fear of God. Men commit sinful acts because they don't believe, in their hearts that, they will be punished for it. God told us, and his word is true, that our sins will destroy, not only the body but the soul. Yet, many go about their acts as if these are just idle words.

I listened to a person on death row talk about her life. She was not angry with the justice system for catching, trying and putting her in prison; on death row. She fully realized it was her life style that brought her there. The way she lived; the things she did, and not having respect for society laws was what led to death row. So, now she had to pay the price for the way she lived. She knew that her death by the law came as a result of her ignoring what it said it would do. It's sad but many people don't realize that their deeds are IOUs to society; and one day society will collect; or pay you; as the case may be.

God program for mankind is no different. He has given us a set of commandments to live by. If we obey the commandments; live them every day, we will be rewarded as promised. If we live in a manner that breaks them we will suffer the things God has promised will come.

Mankind is prone to fear things that will harm the body. But give no thought for the soul. We read the bible, listen to ministers, pastors and other church leaders on truth. We understand that it's wrong to have, or commit sin in any form, yet we don't fear or respect God enough to believe that these acts will destroy our body and soul. Many individuals are in prison today wishing they had a second chance at doing the right thing in society. Many would welcome the chance to return to society and live by society laws. But many will never get that chance. My heart goes out to them; because many never fully understood that their acts were nothing less than disrespect for good and decency.

Fear God! Respect God! He sees your every act. He knows what you are thinking whether good or bad. He knows what is in your heart; your every desire. God sees you twenty fore seven. Your deeds are being recorded. One day you will be faced with your IOUs. Sins and evils are IOUs. Obedient to God's commandments are YOM (you owe me). God will pay you every promise he made. By the same token, you will pay your every IOU.

Mankind sin easily because they do not fear or respect God. They don't fully believe God is going to honor his word, for both good and bad deeds. What do you think will happen if you grab hold of a high power electric line because you don't believe a sign that says it will cause death? Well, God is just as true to his word. Obey and live; disobey and die.

## HOW IS A PERSON DEFILED?

Mathew 15:10-20

:10   And he called the multitude , and said unto them, Hear and understand:

:11 Not that which goeth into the mouth defileth a man; but that which cometh out of the mouth , this deileth a man.

:12 Then came his disciples, and said unto him, knowest thou that the Pharisees were offended, after they heard this saying?

:13 But he answered and said, every plant, which my heavenly Father hath not planted, shall be rooted up.

:14 Let them alone: they be blind leaders of the blind. And if the blind lead the blind, both shall fall into the ditch.

:15 Then answered Peter and said unto him, declare unto us this parable.

:16 And Jesus said, are you also yet without understanding?

:17   Do not ye yet understand that whatsoever entereth in the mouth goeth into the belly, and is caste out into the draught?
:18   But those things which proceed out of the mouth come forth from the heart; and they defile the man.

:19  For out of the heart proceed evil thoughts, murder,

adulteries, fornications, thefts, false witness, blasphemies;

:20   These are the things which defile a man; but to eat with unwashen hands defileth not a man.

Here; Jesus is teaching us how easy it is to fall into traditions and accept them as scripture and truth. As with the scribes and Pharisees that came to Jesus asking why his disciples transgress the tradition of the elders by not washing their hands when they ate. They were not just talking about the Disciples eating with filth on their hands; this hand washing was a sacred thing to them, a ritual to be performed before eating. The main thing to see here is; it was created and taught by the elders, or church leaders. In other words, it was man made. And Jesus let you know in the 13th verse that every man made thing, or tradition, shall be done away with. It's like a gardener keeping his garden free of weeds; if he didn't plant it he will get rid of it.

In today's society many things not scriptural are being accepted as scripture. I find that many church leaders are treating their congregations like politicians treat their constituents; do and say what the majority dictates just to stay in leadership. Modern society leans toward fads and whims; I believe it's now referred to as being politically correct. It changes often, but to remain politically correct you have to change with it. Offend the majority and you are out of their good grace, which means you are out of leadership. So, to stay in power, or keep the position, leaders try to remain politically correct, or let weeds over shadow the main plants.

When Jesus spoke the truth His own disciples worried more about how the ones hearing it felt than about

Jesus speaking it. This is the main point Jesus wants us to see here. In the case of the scribes and Pharisees; they were speaking of violating what they believed was a sacred law; Jesus merely pointed out that this was not a law of God, but something created by man and served no spiritual purpose so He had to get rid of that perception. What you eat is not the problem; rather what you formulate in the heart and produce in words and deeds. These are the things that cause you to violate God's law. Man's law has no relevant with God's law and the two should not be mixed. That's why Jesus made it plain, by telling us to render unto Caesar those thing that are Caesar and unto God those things that are God's.

Slipping into habits, doing things because certain people say it's right, following practices and dictates of an office because it has been placed on a high pedestal by man, knowing the truth and denying it because someone is offended by it, and getting caught up in traditions are very easy to do these days. But, like Jesus, we must adhere to truth through words and deeds. This is the only way to prevent being in violation of God laws. Remember this; the heart is the start of it all. Whether you bless or curse it all comes from the heart. And Jesus looks at the heart, that's why he let us know that we can be guilty of a deed just by committing it in our heart. Remember this; if it's not of God, it will come to naught.

## LET THE WORDS OF MY MOUTH

Psalms 19;14
:14 Let the words of my mouth and the meditations of my heart be acceptable in thy sight O Lord, my strength and my redeemer.

As we move forward in this generation and with the eye opening changes brought upon the people of the United States and the world, and, with the sudden changes in perspectives, let's consider one important thing; "The Words Of Our Mouth."

Whether accepted or not old habits, and ways are hard to change. The disobedience to God's Word; no matter the form; is not going to disappear without sincere efforts on your part to eradicate it with truth and love. Disobedience comes in many forms; hate, lying, envy, lust, fornication, adultery, abuses, addictions, to name a few. And, accepted or not, it is disobedience that shape our actions and form the words we use to interact with people, including close family, each and every day.

The words we speak determine the picture we paint of ourselves for others to see and respond to. Words are a very powerful tool in evoking responses and attitudes. Words can; calm, uplift, encourage, bring joy and happiness, give hope, bless, direct a path, and the list goes on. On the other hand words can; degrade, cast down, bring sadness and hopelessness; cause grief, hate, war and the list goes on.
Words are formed in our hearts through meditating on

175

subjects and issues, and acting on what we meditate about. We think long and hard on a subject and based on what we determine to be our response, we act. When you speak rudely to a person, you have already predetermined, in your heart that you don't like the person or something that person represent or remind you of. Hate and other negatives are no difference. The words you hurl at people match your feelings toward them. Some individuals not only hurl words they exercise physical actions; as with two white males, recently in a small town in Georgia, that brutally attacked a white female for dating a black man. This is a classic case of meditation forming both negative words and actions in the hearts of two men.

These are the things we need to be aware of as we go through changing times. Yes, we are witnessing a growth in unity; church attendance up, more people talking of family unity; people in general expressing a desire to love all people, and many positives signs. but, remember, attending church, loving family and people in general, and doing positive things should come from a sincere desire motivated by love for truth and faith in Jesus Christ. That is why Jesus told us to first seek you the kingdom of heaven and it righteousness because without knowing and accepting the truth about yourself and the people you live and interact with each day, you will not be able to form the words and actions needed to deal with them in a positive manner. If you need to; record your conversation with people for a day, and then sit quietly someplace and listen to yourself; plus write down your true feelings while interaction with the same people and match the two. If it takes a negative event, like a disaster, to make you feel closer to people, then you should ask yourself why. Because that feeling will, in all probability, fade as the event melts into history. Meditate on things that will build lasting words and actions of unity.

Remember, you are your words, or your words are you. As you press forward, your words will paint a vivid picture of you for not only this generation, but future generations to see. Your words and actions are shaping someone, who will believe, speak, and act exactly like you.

The words of your mouth the meditations of your heart are paving a road for someone to follow. Wouldn't it be wonderful if that road led to Jesus Christ.

## A DIVIDED HOUSE  START HERE

Matthew 12:25-26

:25    And Jesus knew their thoughts and said unto them, Every kingdom divided against itself is brought to desolation; and every city or house divided against itself shall not stand:

:26    And if Satan cast out Satan, he is divided against himself; how shall then his kingdom stand?

Here, Jesus is giving us a very strong understanding of unity. They were making a statement but not understanding what they were saying; even though they were just trying to belittle the works of Jesus. But this was

177

done that we might know what will destroy an individual, a family, community, or nation. We were created in the image of God; our soul wants to obey the Word of God. But, when we let our free will, which was also given by God, override the will of the soul and commit an offense against the Word of God we become divided within ourselves. Whether you recognize or just plain ignore it; it is before you daily. You see individuals or groups, wandering from one belief or cause to another. Today they are whooping up one group, tomorrow they are with something totally different. This wandering takes them down many roads, some, even to self destruction. What's happening is they are torn between accepting the desire of the soul to obey God, and exercising the free will which can be influenced by the senses; what we are taught, or learned from others through associations. Regardless of what we become, how we act or what we believe, the soul will always keep before us the obedience of God; it's built in us and will never go away. Yes, we can override it with our freewill, but we will never be satisfied. You may appease yourself by constantly reinforcing the idea that you are happy with; whatever; but if you take a real close look at yourself and accept the facts you will find that you are not happy but a confused person, rejecting your true feelings.

The same principal applies to a family. When two people get married, each one must first be at peace with themselves; that is; have a stable mind. Each one must realize the marriage is based on love only; not physical features like shape, size, or none of the things that will, with time, fade. When a union is formed in love, whatever is brought forth from it will be a product of love; whether children, wealth, or goods. And when these things are a product of love they will never become a replacement for love, nor will physical changes minimize love. Many marriages end in divorce because of physical changes in size features, or financial status. "Some ends because of children being born, or the needs of children are seen as a burden. There are many, many more, but they are all outside of love. Individuals and groups commit horrendous acts against their own communities or nations because, first, they are not at peace with themselves and second, their wandering mind uses something they have learned or been taught, to try and appease itself. It's not stability. The word of God is stable because it is truth and love you can depend on.

Jesus is telling us plainly if we want unity, come together in love and truth. That's why he told us truth shall set us free. He also told us not to build our foundation on sand, because it shifts, or moves; it's not stable; the Word of God is; because it's truth and love. You can depend on it. It will never change.

You can be strong; your family strong and united, your marriage sure, if you build on love. Never let the word compatibility, enter your marriage. That word always refers to a changeable characteristic that will surely fade with time.

Stop, meditate, and listen to the soul as it speaks to your heart. Compare your thinking to the Word of God; if you have doubts of what you are hearing. Remember, the desires of your soul will never go away; it wants to obey God. If your free will dictates something else, you are a divided house.

You will never find total peace, no mater what you gain in this world, until your free will is in harmony with the desire of the soul.

## WE ARE BLESSED

I John 3:1-3

:1 Behold what manner of love the Father has bestowed on us, that we should be called the sons of God! Therefore the world knoweth us not because it knew him not.
:2 Beloved, now we are the sons of God; and it does not yet appear what we shall be; but we know that when he shall appear, we shall be like him for we shall see him as he is.
:3 And every man that hath this hope in him purifieth himself, even as he is pure.

Have you ever known anyone who just wanted to be a part of a family because of what that family stood for? Have you ever experienced it yourself? I have. There was this family, in my young life, that I thought was so great and doing such great things I just wanted to be a part of what they were doing. For a time I did become a part of what they were doing and I felt great about myself and what I was involved in. I have always felt that helping people better their lives are the greatest help humans can extend to one another. But, it takes love to do it. Look at the reality Jesus is sharing with us here. God, who can bring anything into being by speaking it; who is holy, true, and almighty; is saying to us; who have been and may still be sinning; you are my children. That in itself should make you shout, because God is saying, "I love you, I want the very best for you and I will give you the best.

Parents wants the best for their children, And they work hard to give them the best. God lets us know that from the foundation of the earth, I prepared wonderful things for you and I want you to have them. But, like any household, there are rules to follow. And in order for us to have all that the Father has prepared we must follow the rules that is clearly laid out for us. Example: parents say to the children, there will be no drugs, alcohol drinking, smoking and wild parties in our home. If you do, you will be cut off from this family and thrown out with those you committed these acts with. But, the child decides to break the rules and do these things anyway. Well, the child will suffer the punishment that the parents said would come as a result of breaking house rules. Sure the children wild partying friends may not understand or even accept the children refusal to break their parent's rules, but the children know the benefit of being obedience and choose it rather than be disobedience and brings on the wrath of the parents.

Following the teaching of Jesus; that is, being obedience to the Word; you will certainly be misunderstood by many, some may be close friends. But you understand God through His Holy Word and you know the benefits of obedience and understand and know the wrath of disobedience. You also know that it is better to please God than have a pat on the back by man.

The other great reality is we pay no attention to

Joseph Haugabrook

pictures and images man have come up with trying to show what God looks like. We know that God is love. We know that He is Holy. We know that His Word is true. And, we know we are a part of His perfect plan. So we know because we are obedience to His Word, we are and will continue to be like Him. We also know that His Word flowing through our thoughts and motivating our actions purifies us like the perfect filter filtering out contaminates from water. We truly understand that the pictures seen hanging on walls and displayed in many areas are just another way man is trying to bolster his own vain ego or importance. We fully understand the vainness of this effort; that it does not in anyway depict God. It is just another one of Satan's tricks to divide people and minimize the unity of God's family.

We are truly blessed to be called children, by God. I rejoice just thinking about it. Because, I know, being a child of God, I can ask for any good thing He has placed on this earth and will receive it. I don't have to doubt whether I will receive, what I ask for. I know, because being obedient to His Word I will maintain the proper frame of mind both while asking and after receiving.


## WHAT YOU GET FOR STAYING WITH JESUS; WHAT YOU LOSE BY LEAVING

John 15:5-7

:5 I am the vine, you are the branches. He that abides in me and I in him the same bringeth forth much fruit; for without

182

Me you can do nothing.

:6  If a man abide not in Me, he is cast forth as a branch and is withered; and men gather them and cast them into the fire and they are burned.

:7  If ye abide in Me and My words abide in you, ye shall ask what you will, and it shall be done unto you.

In the seventh verse Jesus says to us: If you believe in Me; trust in Me, live the way I tell you to live, let your words be kind and loving to those you interact with, be positive and encouraging, be honest and truthful, put the programs of God above all else, fast and pray; do these things and whatever you desire you will receive, because by doing this you are bearing fruit; that is, your deeds and actions are showing others what happens when one lives as the Bible say live. And, God is being glorified by your actions and deeds. To put it another way, when your actions and deeds, mirrors what Jesus taught and lived on earth, you become a shining example of what God want in his children. You become a tree with big beautiful fruit that anyone can eat, live and not starve. Plainly, you become the fleshy example for people to live by. You live by the Word; you get the promises of the Word.

The ending of the fifth verse says plainly; without me you can do nothing.
Jesus tells us plainly: Look at the vine, the sap flows from the root to every branch on the vine. When a branch is cut off, it falls to the ground, withers and is burned. The branch is totally dependent on the vine. The branch cannot become

fruitful without the vine. There are no way men and women can live a life that mirrors what Jesus taught without the Word of God molding and shaping all actions and deeds. You cannot have real love without real love in your heart. You can't be truthful without truth in your heart. You cannot believe and trust in God without knowing the Word of God. You cannot resist the lures of sin without the power of God strengthening you. You only have to look at the decay of morality in America and other countries to see that reality. When you let love, honesty, truth, understanding, and all the positives, shown in the bible, shape what you say and do, not only will your needs be provided, your desires will be as well. All these things will be given you in this life and the life to come. on the other hand if you decide to go it on your own; guess what; you are not on your own, because the enemy, old Satan, is right there to grab hold of the reins and lead you his way; all the while making you think you are doing it on your own, and, it's the right way to go and right thing to do. In present times it's called politically correct that is, making what man has determined correct, your way of responding to people places and things. To put it plainly, you can have all the riches, comforts, and peace God placed on this earth, and eternal life, if you live your life according to the teachings of Jesus. You can have the pains, fears, frustration, inner and outer wars, and all the negatives of society, plus lose your soul by rejecting the teaching of Jesus; it's up to you.

Let's Talk About Jesus

## WHEN YOU PRAY

John 16:21-29

:21  A woman when she is in travail hath sorrow. because her hour is come: but as soon as she is delivered of the child, she remembereth no more the anguish, for joy that a man is born into the world.

:22  And ye now therefore have sorrow: but I will see you again, and your heart shall rejoice, and your joy no man taketh from you.

:23  And in that day ye shall ask me nothing. Verily, verily, I say unto you, Whatsoever ye shall ask the Father in my name, he will give it you.

:24  Hithreto have ye asked nothing in my name: ask, and ye shall receive, that your joy may be full.

:25  These things have I spoken unto you in proverbs: but the time cometh, when I shall no more speak unto you in proverbs, but I shall shew you plainly of the Father.

:26  At that day ye shall ask in my name: and I say not unto you, that I will pray the Father for you:

:27  For the Father himself  loveth you, because ye have love me, and have believed that I came out from God.

:28    I came forth from the Father, and am come into the world: again, I leave the world, and go to the Father.

:29    His disciples said unto him, Lo, now speakest thou plainly, and speakest no proverb.

You already know from past teachings that all prayers must be sincere and with unwavering faith. You believe in the Father. You believe that Jesus is the Son of God and that He came to earth in the flesh and suffered the punishments of our sins and redeemed us through His pure Holy Blood. That is, Jesus, being in the flesh, like you and I, subject to all the temptations as you and I, yet did not yield to any; or did not sin. We know and understand that it took pure love for God to send His son on our behalf, and it took pure love for Jesus to willingly go through such an ordeal. So, knowing all this we fully believe and trust in the Words now compiled into what we know as the bible. We fully believe that these Words are our instruction on how to live in this world and to gain eternal life in the world to come. There is no question about this, but there is a question, by some, of whether to pray to Jesus or the Father. Yes, the Father, son and Holy Ghost are one; but don't interject that here. Jesus, as he is speaking to the disciples; is explaining to us the way to pray.

Prayer, as you well know, is our way of talking to God about any concern, care, need or desire we may have. When Jesus died on the cross and the veil of the temple was rent, or torn in half, opening the way to the Holiest of Holy, each individual on this earth, at that instant, through the Blood of Jesus, was now able to go to the Father, on his or her own behalf. Individuals no longer needed an earthly being to go to the Father for them; every individual now goes to the Father in prayer, for the things he or she wants from God.

How is this done? Simple! Pray to God in the name of Jesus.

Do not be deceived; pray in the name of Jesus. Talk to God in plain simple language. You don't need men so called, impressive words. You don't need long prayers filled with vain words; that are to impress another human being. If you desire God to strengthen your faith, just ask God to strengthen you faith, in the name of Jesus. In other words, you are going through Jesus to ask for what it is you are seeking from God. You are going into the Holiest of Holy to place your request on the altar, but instead of going through a veil, which was once the door to the to the Holiest of Holy, you are going through Jesus who is now the door to the Holiest of holy.

In verses 24-27 Jesus speaks plainly without parables. Verse 24, Jesus says plainly that never before did anyone have to pray to the Father in His name. In verse 26 you note that Jesus is saying plainly that in the day He fulfills all things; that is, when he give up the Ghost on the cross, from that moment, we, every human being on earth, will have to pray to God in his name, the name of Jesus. This is not negotiable. It is not to be questioned. Jesus is saying I will not pray for you, praying is your responsibility. But if you want the Father to honor your prayer, pray to him in My name doubting 'nothing. Remember, this is not about any congregational name, or, as man put it, religion. This apply to every human being; period.

Those are the rules! Pray in the name of Jesus, fully

believing that Jesus is the son of God and he suffered on earth in the flesh and that he returned to the Father and is now at the right hand of the father. Jesus will not pray for us, but he will intercede on our behalf when we make an honest mistake in our sincere prayer.

## EASY AND SIMPLE

John 6:26-29

:26   Jesus answered them and said, Verily, verily, I say unto you, ye seek me, not because ye saw the miracles, but because ye did eat of the loaves, and were filled.

:27   Labour not for the meat which perisheth, but for that meat which endureth unto everlasting life, which the son of man shall give unto you: for him hath God the Father sealed.
:28   Then said they unto him, what shall we do, that we might work the works of God?

:29   Jesus answered and said unto them, This is the work of God, that ye believe on him whom he hath sent.

Jesus is pointing out the reason people become a part of a group or congregation using His name, not just the ones with Him then, but people of today as well. Jesus had just performed a great miracle before these people and they were looking for Him again, not because of the miracle, but because they were seeking to satisfy a fleshy need. That is; to satisfy the yearning of the flesh. That old song, stealing in the name of the Lord, holds true. Many join churches with the explicit reason of fleshy gains. Jesus is telling us not to come to Him looking for things that only please the yearning of the flesh. Jesus calls such; things that perish. What Jesus wants us to do is look at His work, the miracles that He performed. Look at His attitude or disposition while performing the miracles. Example: Jesus had deep compassion for people following Him to hear and understand the Word of God. They wanted to understand and become a part of what Jesus was teaching. While they were doing it a need for food arose; so much so that Jesus said if we send them away they will faint by the wayside. In other words they are too hungry and weak to keep going, especially trying to hunt for food. So, having love and compassion for their needs; Jesus fed them. He will provide for us in like manner. Every miracle Jesus performed has a lesson in it for us. And the two I want to point out here is: when you come to Jesus don't let that car, house, bank account, or any selfish need be the motivation. Have a sincere desire to learn more about what Jesus is teaching and to become a part of it. Note verse 28. The people asked Jesus, what they had to do to work the works of God. In other words, what did they have to do to be obedient to God? Jesus answered them in simple terms; Believe in Mim whom God had sent; this is the second lesson in these scriptures. Again, push fleshy yearning aside and truly believe in Jesus and the works He did on earth.

So, looking at the works of Jesus, we see clearly what we have to do to satisfy God. The important thing to instill in self is; believe in Jesus! Believe His every Word, look at His attitude, and believe the miracles He performed and let your attitude, disposition, and deeds, mirror those of

Jesus.

If all your works on this earth is to satisfy the yearning of the flesh then, your works will, someday perish, and so will you.

God loves you and want you to be obedient to His Word. God's plan was laid out from the foundation of the world and will not change because of the whims of mankind. I've said it before and I'm saying it again; God's Word is not hard to understand. The mystery of the word which many find confusing is how the Word of God can, in itself, create thing out of nothing. The mystery is how a few fish and barley loaves can be stretched to feed thousands. Some, because they don't see the actual force that is making more fish or bread, call it a mystery. You don't have to do that; just accept it as it is; the works of God fulfilling the needs of His people. And God doesn't need anything created by man to make it happen. Look at his first miracle, when he turned water into wine. Jesus put his miracle into man made vessels; because man and his objects are the beneficiaries of God's blessings; but not the maker; man certainly didn't make water.

Seek Jesus for spiritual enrichment, and believe that He is the Son of God and that God sent Him to restore things as it was in the beginning. Know also that this was done through great suffering in the flesh and death on the cross. If you believe in Him you will trust Him and be obedient to all His teachings. And just like the multitude got their needs fulfilled without knowing Jesus was going to do it; your needs will likewise be fulfilled.

Let's Talk About Jesus

## LET NOT YOUR HEART BE TROUBLED

John 14:1

:1 Let not your heart be troubled; you believe in God, believe also in me.

I do so because it is important to understand how easy it is for what may seem an innocent act, to become a life altering deed with a life time effect. Christmas; think about it. This is a time of year when thoughts turns to one thing. Giving and receiving. From Thanksgiving to the New Year an aura, not experienced at any other time of year, emanate from seemingly, everyone. The stores are crowded; streets are jammed with traffic, creating, many times, rage and violence. Shoppers, grabbing and snatching items they want to purchase; drivers honking, gesturing and worse, because of slow moving traffic and the list goes on. With all of this, it is only the tip of the iceberg. Christmas day: the culmination of all the frustration of buying for one day of giving and receiving.

And yes, some bad things happen during this time: robbing, killing, stealing, fighting, cursing, threatening, incarceration and more. It has happened in the past, it will happen again in the future, unless we heed the Word of God. Some will look at what has been given to them and right away form a negative attitude that can and have led to life long hate for the giver. The attitudes of: he or she could have given me more, or a better gift that this! Or, I wouldn't have given my worst enemy this mess; or, I gave them this and they gave me this thing! Or, the gift is nice but ole (whatever the name) is just showing off because, he or she, has a little money! Or, children saying, I wanted that, not this ole thing. And the list goes on.

The great evil in all this is; humanity becomes so involved, so caught up in the idea of giving and receiving, that the real reason for celebrating this one day event, "The birth of Jesus" is completely forgotten. Jesus is taken out of the equation. I don't decry giving, but I do the attitudes it creates. If what is given in love is not received in the same manner, it becomes evil on the part of the receiver. Because of a perishable item people lose friendship, become enemies, and, in some cases maim, murder, and suffer the results of these acts. So, ask yourself; is it worth it? (Please note I'm not saying don't give) The facts I would like you to look at during the season is: God's gift to mankind was, love. God loved mankind so much that He didn't want mankind to remain outside of the perfect plan He had originally laid out for him. So, the only way to reenter God's perfect plan was through atonement by pure blood; the blood of flesh without spot or wrinkle; in other word flesh that had never sinned. Jesus, through love, became that flesh and by the will of God, was born through flesh (Mary). Peace on earth, good will toward men, became a reality for mankind through the love of the Father and Son. What we must keep in mind is; this was a gift of love. It was given to everyone and it benefited everyone equally. The giver wasn't put in the poor house, didn't borrow, steal rob or the like to give the gift. The heavens rejoiced; didn't become troubled because of the gift.

You may say; but some on earth became troubled. And I will hasten to say you are exactly right. But, why were they troubled? Because the gift; Jesus Christ; became a perceived threat to the status quo. Not a real threat, but a perceived threat. The attitude: "I'm going to lose my power, my status, my control, and other worldly lusts. This is the same attitude that has contaminated the celebration of Jesus' birth. I have to have money to buy a gift, so I won't look bad as parents, a friend, and a sib, or be thought of as being too poor to buy anything. The attitude then, become personal, an ego, not a part of the season.

Why get angry over what you receive? Why get angry over not receiving an item, whether a card or something else? Why take pride or be boastful in a perishable item you want to give or worry over what you can't afford to give? God didn't make giving gifts a requirement to rejoice over the birth of Jesus, nor to interact among one another. The gift was love. Jesus commandment to us is love. And love should be given each day. It should be a part of our daily interaction with one another; just as Jesus, our gift from God.

Will your gift show love? I will leave that decision to you because as long as the gift is given in love, not spite; is affordable, will not, now or later, take away from an obligation, will help not hurt, is capable of creating a positive in daily living, then by all means give. But, give from your abundance, what you have and can afford; not from what you have to create and obligation to do.

Whether accepted or not, worrying is having a troubled heart, and, having a troubled heart is worrying. So, since Jesus has told us not to do either, we disobey his word when we do. The season should create in you the same feelings and hopes brought to God's children the day Jesus was born. Your heart should rejoice, not be troubled in any way.

## YOU WILL SEE IT AGAIN

Revelation 20:12

:12  And I saw the dead; small and great, stand before God; and the books were opened; and another book was opened, which is the book of life; and the dead were judged out of those things which were written in the books, according to their works.

This is plain and to the point. We are going to be judged, in the Day of Judgment, according to what is written in the books. The deeds of our lives are being recorded, deed by deed. And, these deeds are going to determine whether Jesus will say "Well done, or depart from me." That is both frightening and joyous. If you live according to the Word of God, that day will be joyous. If not, then it's frightening. Joyous because you know you will spend eternal life with Jesus Christ. Frightening because you know you will be eternally damned. It's a frightening thought to think of spending eternity in hell. But, if you don't love people in general, help in whys you can, be kind, respectful, understanding, cooperative, refrain from lust, greed, lying, and the like, you are planting seeds, or doing deeds, that will send you to eternal damnation.

Let's Talk About Jesus

The important thing to remember is: when you face the things written in the Books, you will not be able to deny them, because you will know that you did them. Everything you do in this life is being recorded, just like you take a tape recorder and record a program or music from another tape or disk. You are going to remember each deed as it happen, in the Day of Judgment.

There is nothing in this life you can gain to save you except holiness; that is, believe Jesus is the Son of God and live your life according to His Word. To live His Word, you have to learn what it says, whether reading or listening to it from one of God's servants. It is like Jesus said, truth will set you free. His word is truth so learn it, live it and you will become free indeed. As you go through each day, keep in mind the things you do are being written down and you will have to face them again. What would you like for them to be?

## WHEN YOU WILLINGLY ACCEPT JUSUS

John 6:15-21

:15  When Jesus therefore perceived that they would come and take him by force, to make him a king, he departed again into a mountain himself alone.

:16  And when even was now come, his disciples went down unto the sea,

:17   And entered into a ship and went over the sea toward Capernaum, and it was now dark and Jesus was not come to them.

:18   And the sea arose by reason of a great wind that blew.

:19   So when they had rowed about five and twenty or thirty furlongs, they see Jesus walking on the sea, and drawing nigh unto the ship: and they were afraid.

:20   But he saith unto them, It is I; be not afraid.

:21   Then they willingly received him into the ship: and immediately the ship was at the land whither they went.

There are three important things to look at here: first, the sea; second, the actions of the disciples; third, what Jesus said and what took place after the Disciples accepted Him into the boat.

The Disciples had taken a boat and was rowing their way toward Capernaum, but a strong wind caused the sea to be rough, which made their job  difficult; at best. It's safe to say, they were going no where. It was dark and they see someone coming to them walking on water. Naturally they became afraid. But Jesus spoke, confirming it was Him and ask them not to be afraid. The disciples believed Jesus and willingly accepted Him in the boat. Immediately after Jesus got on board, the boat was at land where they were trying to reach.

With all the troubles in the world today; with all the problems facing individuals and families, it's comforting to know there is a solution; the above scriptures show it plainly.

Like the Disciples we start our day with hope; or we start our career with expectation, only to find that something pops up bring in trouble, trials and all kinds of problems, making our efforts, at best, very difficult. I listen daily to leaders around the world proclaiming peace, while waging war. I see husbands and wives saying they want a loving family, while at odds with each other and the list goes on. You know yourself how sometimes you set out to do a task only to find something popping up to try and stop what you are trying to do, or at least make it very difficult.

The Disciples were trying very hard to row in a strong wind and high seas. They saw something; it was Jesus; they believed His words and without doubt accepted Him into the boat and they made it safe to land; immediately.

Like the Disciples you may be struggling with what may seem an impossible problem, but if you trust the Words of Jesus and accept them into you life; making them a part of your efforts, your problems will be solved.

Can you see why the Disciples were afraid? They are battling a rough sea and here comes a man walking on it. Sure they were afraid so would any person. But, when Jesus spoke, they believed Him, even the miracle He was performing before their eyes; walking on water. Just alike Jesus came to them in the rough sea, and fixed their problem, whatever problem you are facing He is right where you can see Him; if you look and not be afraid to trust and believe.

Jesus is speaking to us through His Words today,

197

asking that we be not afraid to trust Him. If we heed his Words we already have the solution to whatever problem we are facing. Don't try and use Jesus as you would an automobile mechanic; only call him when something goes wrong with the car (in our case, in our lives), he doesn't work that way. The way to peace, in the home, community and nation is to willingly accept Jesus in your life. Sure, on the surface it may seem impossible, that just accepting Jesus into your life will solve the problem you are facing. But do like the Disciples did; trust his Words.

## IF JESUS WAS HERE

John 11:21-27

:21   Then said Martha unto Jesus, Lord, if thou hadst been here, my brother had not died.

:22   But I know, that even now, whatsoever thou wilt ask of God, God will give it thee.

:23   Jesus saith unto her, Thy brother shall rise again.

:24   Martha saith unto him, I know that he shall rise again in the resurrection at the last day.

:25   Jesus said unto her, I am the resurrection, and the life: he that believeth in me though he were dead, yet shall he live:

:26   And whosoever liveth and believeth in Me shall never die. Believest thou this?

:27   She saith unto him, Yea, Lord: I believe that thou art the Christ, the Son of God, which should come into the world.

This is a prime example of how easy it is to let ourselves become focused on physical presence. There in no doubt Martha knew Jesus and the miracles he had performed to that date. But, in the case of her brother, she felt that Jesus presence was required while Lazarus was still alive to heal him, or keep him alive.

Martha's response is not a great mystery, it's not rare at all to find faith being pushed aside for physical presence. That is, believing more in what can be seen, touched, tasted, or smelled; than in Jesus, whom we don't see in the physical and forget that he is present. In my travel and intermingling with people across this and several foreign countries, I have seen many that say they believe in Jesus, yet seek palmist, and the like, for what they call spiritual guidance; and mainly because they can see and/or converse with these people. This is not to criticize the ones doing it; it is to point up how easy it is to forget that Jesus is present at all times, but we must be patience and let him perform His perfect will at the time appointed. Jesus knew about Lazarus sickness and death; but He waited until the time appointed to give again to Lazarus the gift of life. There are things we want or desire in this life; but we have to exercise patience and faith to get them. Martha wanted her brother to live. She wanted to be able to enjoy his physical present as she had done over his life time. And when Jesus told her it would happen again, her mind had slipped from the present to the resurrection. We sometimes forget that Jesus wants us to enjoy the beauty and riches of this world just as He wants us to someday enjoy the glorious things with Him in Heaven. Jesus didn't put the beauty and riches of the earth here to make us miserable; but to enjoy. We sometimes forget that God's Blessings are already in place for us, and all we have to do is align our lives with the Word of God to receive them. When you want, and ask Jesus for a blessing, have faith that it's coming and have the patience to wait. Praying to Jesus for something and not having the patience to wait is like having your child come to you asking for a dollar; and you being a little slow in reaching into your pocket or wallet and handing it to him or her, and they stomp off saying they will get it some other way. Chances are that child will miss out on the dollar, maybe more than you were going to give them.

We don't see the wind, or the power contained therein, but we do see and feel the results. God is a spirit, we don't see his physical form, but we do see the power of His might. We can look at the sun and moon, knowing that throughout the centuries, it has never failed to give its light as appointed. It is a part of God's program; it's perfect, sure, and can be relied on. We can rely on the Word of Jesus. Don't let the word "if" become a part of your thinking when it comes to your faith and patience in Jesus.

## WALK IN THE LIGHT

Matthews 5:14-16

:14  Ye are the light of the world. A city that is set on an hill cannot be hid

:15   Neither do men light a candle, and put it under a bushel, but on a candlestick; and it giveth light unto all that are in the house.

:16   Let your light so shine before men that they may see your good works, and glorify your Father which is in heaven.

Please understand that the point given here is very important because it is giving a clear view of the power God has instilled in each of us if we choose to accept and use it. Those that understand and use the word of God in conducting the affairs of life are a powerful force of righteousness that cannot be overshadowed by the forces working against the teachings of Jesus. Look at the 15th verse; once God's word is accepted and practiced in all interactions with people, places and things, God will not allow it to be hidden from anyone. It will be in plain view to be seen by everyone; and its reality cannot be denied. It can be ignored by those who choose to do so, but it cannot be hidden.

I don't care who you are, where you came from, or what you do or believe in, built into you is the desire to be obedient to God. That obedience; following God's Word; is the light that you show to mankind. Given to you is the option to accept or reject this obedience. In other words, God let every human being decide whether or not to accept His teachings. He tells us what will happen if we follow His teachings and what will happen if we reject his teachings. Examples are given throughout the bible.

Here, Jesus is showing us the power we have to lead

those that don't understand into a full understanding of truth and righteousness. Look at Jesus Words; the salt of the earth; the light of the world. He's talking about you. In you is the desire to obey and that desire is the light or understanding that will show mankind the true meaning of God's wWord so that they can use it in their daily interaction with nouns.

When you walk in the light; that is; be obedient and not reject the teachings of Jesus, whether you know it or not, you are setting examples that many will see and follow. Yes, there will be those that will continue to reject their built-in obedience; but the job of the obedient ones is to hold fast to what they are doing without judging in any way. Those that reject let them reject. Those that accept let them accept. Jesus doesn't force His word on the obedient and the obedient shouldn't force God's Word or their effort on anyone. The light you have; stand and hold it high and steady. Smile at those that laugh at you. Bless those that criticize you. Pray for those that do evil against you. No matter what come against you hold your light with a firm grip and steady hand; Meaning; in your interaction with people, places and things, don't waiver in sharing, being truthful, honest, helpful, cooperative, loving and positive.

Isn't it amazing how the forces of darkness are drawing in so many; making them stumble about in darkness; rather than stay in the light where they can see their way? Think of this as you go about your efforts to earn daily bread; salt preserve; light exposes the obstacles that causes one to stumble.

Let's Talk About Jesus

## WHO DO YOU BELIEVE JESUS IS?

Matthew 16:13-16

:13   When Jesus came into the coasts of Caesarea Philippi he asked his disciples, saying, Whom do men say that I the son of man am?
:14   And they said, Some say that thou are John the Baptist: some, Elias; and others, Jeremias or one of the prophets.

:15   He saith unto them, But whom say ye that I am?

:16 And Simon Peter answered and said, Thou are the Christ, the Son of the living God.

These passages of scriptures points up a very important need in our lives. Jesus is showing us that it is not what others say, but what we truly believe that affects our lives. Someone can warn you of a quicksand pit in your path, but if you truly don't believe them you will walk right into it. We act and react on what we truly believe. Jesus knew the answer to the question He asked the Disciples, but his question made the Disciples take note of their own beliefs. Look at the question. What are others saying and believe about me? Look at the answer. You are the Christ, the son of the living God.

The Disciples were not paying attention to what others were saying; positive or negative. Their full attention was on what Jesus was saying and doing. And, by so doing they were able to see the greatness on His work. The love He was demonstrating for all people; in short they could see the

Godliness in Him and His works.

The scripture Jesus gave us is very much needed in these times of so much talk and differences among men. There is different thinking as to what Jesus really represents to mankind. There is different thinking as to what the Holy Bible really teaches mankind. And certainly there is different thinking as to what is and is not Holy and Righteous. Today; as in the time when Jesus walked the earth, thinking and practices are all over the place. Some people sitting in the same congregation, listening to the same pastor, year after year, think different from others sitting in the same congregation. And this applies both to those saying they are serving Jesus and those serving the other god they choose. In short, different thinking, about the same thing exists in every facet of our lives. So, it is important to stop and look at what you really believe; and what you are truly acting on each day, because that is what will affect your life; and, how Jesus sees you each day.

Jesus is reinforcing the fact that it is not what others say and do, it is what we say and do, that determines whether we are blessed or damned. We are not blessed by what others say about, or do to us; but rather what we do to and say about others. We can't love God without first loving those around us. We can't be obedient to Gods Word without first fulfilling His commandment to treat those around us as He treats us. So, it's very important to look at what we really think and believe about Jesus. You have to look deep to see if He is really real in your heart. If you truly believe He is the Son of the living God. If you truly believe all power is in His hands. If He truly has the answers to your problem, if you truly believe, then you will not take note of what is being said and done by others, but, what truly is in your heart. You must know you will not find Jesus sitting among hate, envy, adultery, immoral acts, lying, cheating or any negative. So, if you have any negatives about God's creations in your heart, then you will not find Jesus among them. In other Words if you heart is filled with negatives, don't look for Jesus there. Just remember you act and react to what's in your heart; because that is what you truly believe.

## WE ARE NOT PERFECT, JUST FORGIVEN

Ephesians 4:31-32
:31    Let all bitterness, and wrath, and anger, and clamour, and evil speaking be put away from you, with all malice:

:32 And be ye kind one to another, tenderhearted, forgiving one another, even as God for Christ's sake hate forgiven you.

The scriptures are straight forward and to the point. It's easy to accomplish. However, you can fall into a rut or let something become a habit; even then it's easy to get rid of by turning to Jesus for guidance. That is; learn God's Word and conduct you life according to what it says. I know you've heard this before; I have many times. "You are what you have been taught, learned and practiced. Those three make up your thinking, decisions and actions. Learning to hate someone because of a physical characteristic is a classic example. You can hear so many negative things about a person, place, or thing that your decisions and actions are totally based on what you have heard. On my first trip to Florida, I was driving alone, on highway 95, and well into the state by nine o'clock. It was dark, and on either side of the highway was forest. I was praying that my car didn't break down or I had a flat tire, because I had always heard that there were lots of alligators in Florida, and to me those forests were nothing but swamps filled with alligators that would very likely attack me if I had to leave the car for any reason. Whether true or false, to me it was reality.

You hear so many different things about people, about the Word of God, about society in which you live; and summations of what it all means, and why this or that should or should not be accepted. In short, confusion ranges supreme in everything that touches your life. That is why it is so important that you have one source that has proven itself through the ages, to draw on. It doesn't matter what has been or will be said about the word of God, no one can dispute, that the Bible, the Word of God, is the best way to live a peaceful loving and successful life. No one can truthfully deny that the bible is the book to live by. So it's a good thing to make what it says a part of your life and the life of your children. There is no such thing as people can't live together in love and peace. We have the blue print to do it. But, because of teachings and practices it's ignored.

Look at the scriptures above; just try what it is saying until you rid yourself of just the things it's telling you not to do. I know you will feel better spiritually, mentally and physically. Your life will change and you will have those things that will give you comfort, peace and serenity. In short your needs will be met, because you will have aligned your life with the Word of God; the pathway to all blessings.

## STRONG IN YOUR PLACE OF WORSHIP; WEAK OUTSIDE

Jonah 4:1-2
(Read all 4 Chapters)

:1 Now the Word of the Lord came to Jonah the son of A-mi-tai saying,

:2 Arise, go to Nineveh, that great city, and cry out against it: for their wickedness has come up before me.

When you read the 4 chapters of Jonah, note Jonah's attitude, and you will understand how it affected others. Which will also let you understand how you; disobeying God's commandments; affect others.

Jonah's attitude was, by his own admission, he really didn't see any reason why he should go to Nineveh to take God's Word to the people of the city, because God was going to forgive them anyway. Chapter 4, verse 1 & 2 Trying to out guess God is what gets us into trouble. God gave us a talent that can help others, but we don't want to use it, or we want to do what we want to with it. God knows what He's doing, and we should follow His instructions, because it will always help somebody.

Jesus has given you exactly what he knows you can

accomplish, so there's no excuse for not accomplishing it. Your strength for doing God's work lies in your heart. That is; think, live, and practice the Word of God to the letter. You can read the life of Moses, and note how God reminded him to follow His instructions exactly, in building the temple or the Ark of the Covenant. Nothing could be added or taken away. Why? Because that was a shadow of things already in God's program of eternity. In other words, those measurements and adornments are a small, but exact scale of thing already existing from the foundation of the world. And God is not going to change it because we don't want to follow instructions.

Our gift of prosperity on earth; love, peace, riches, and all the positives in this life; and eternal life to come; is already prepared, and the path to it already laid. But, we have to follow, to the letter, God's instructions to reach it. The way is not going to change; the instructions are not going to be amended; as the saying goes; what you see is what you get; take it or leave it; it's your option. God gave you that right. Of course, I urge you to follow instruction and not fall into the pit of hell just outside the given path.

This is not to say, don't express your true feeling of thankfulness to Jesus openly. Just let the Word guide your expressions in and out of congregations. If you sincerely read, understand, and live by the Word of God, your actions and reactions will not change no matter where you are or what event you encounter. When a driver cut you off, you won't cuss. When someone jump in front of you in a long line where you have been standing for a long time, you won't start and argument or fight. When someone put pressure on you to do something you knows is not in accordance with the teachings of Jesus, you will not do it. In other word, you are doing what God told Peter, James and John on the mountain of transfiguration's this is my beloved son, hear him.

Remember, your weakness, as explained in the churches in Revelation, is always before you, Satan will see to that; but, in those churches, are your strengths and how to overcome your weaknesses. Read them all, over and over again, and when you find yourself, read it continuously. Never let yourself be caught short by thinking I have this; I'm alright. In Christ; the Word of God; I am strengthened against all evils. On my own I can do nothing; through Jesus I can do all things.

## DENYING JESUS

St. John 13:36-38

:36 Simon Peer said unto Him. Lord, whither goes thou? Jesus answered, whither I go, thou canst not follow me now; but thou shalt follow me afterwards.

:37 Peter said unto him, Lord, why cannot I follow thee now? I will lay down my life for thy sake.

Question; would you deny Jesus? I fully believe Peter was sincere when he said he would lay down his life for Jesus' sake. At that moment, I believe he meant it with every fiber of his being. But, when he feared for his life, he not only denied knowing Jesus, he cursed while doing it. Jesus had already told Peter that: before the cock crows you will deny me three times. So, will you, or have you, ever denied Jesus? Remember Jesus knows what we are going to do before we do it. We don't always know, but Be does, so be honest with you.

There have been times in my younger life, when I went to church and felt, during the service, that I could conquer the world. My feelings would be so strong that I felt there was nothing in the world could make me commit an offense against the Word of God. I was strong, I believed, I had faith! Yet, during the week, when I was faced with problems; something going wrong on the job, money low, debts high, need but didn't have, children acting up and the list goes on; I forgot the strong feelings I had in church, I went for what I thought would solve the problem and it was all man made solutions. In short, I leaned to my own experiences and understanding. I trusted in what I thought was the solution; and, it was not Jesus.

When something threatening rear its ugly head, it's very easy to lie, or do things that will appease someone else, just to make it go away. Peter's life was threatened, and he loved life, so, he felt by saying he didn't know Jesus, whom he felt was sure to be put to death, he would not be charged with what Jesus was being charged with, thereby being able to live. Peter was doing what so many did before him and many are doing right now; lying to save his life. I believe the new phrase is; protecting my hide, or saving myself. Some even call it doing what's best for me and my family. It's amazing how many sins are committed in the name of saving self and family.

As you interact with nouns, it's good to ask yourself; am I doing what's popular or what's right according to the word of Jesus? Are you ashamed to do those things Jesus said we should do? Am I loving like He said love? It's not how we feel in church; it's how we react when faced with troubles. In the present of other church goers, we may feel like we can move mountains, but what happens in the present of non-believers, when a mountain needs moving? You know the answer to that question, and you know what your reactions are or will be.

You will likely face problems and difficulties in the future; so how are you going to handle them? Please take a close look at "Just doing whatever is necessary to cover self" before acting. Doing whatever is necessary could be a move of denial.

## WE CAN PERSECUTE JESUS BY NOT KNOWING THE TRUTH

Acts 9:4

:4 Then he fell to the grown and heard a voice saying to him, "Saul, Saul, why persecutest thou me?

We see in this scripture, Saul, who later became Paul, thought with all his heart that he was doing the work of God by trying to destroy, what he thought of as a sect against the law. Saul deeds and actions caused the destruction of many who believed and lived the life outlined by Jesus. This is not to condemn Saul, but look at your own deeds and actions and compare them to the examples Jesus gave throughout the New Testament for us to follow and see if what you are doing is in line with what Jesus said to do.

I have, laying beside me, a template for different size drill bits. It is a series of holes starting with a large hole and going down to a very small one. Underneath each hole is the bit size needed to drill that size hole. I don't have to guess about the size bit I need to drill a certain size hole. I just compare the template to the hole I feel I need. I can also lay the template over a hole to determine what size it is and whether or not I have the size hole for the intended purpose. Jesus teachings shows us exactly, without guess work, what is needed to accomplish his intended purpose for our life. Jesus had a purpose for Saul's life, but he had to make Saul see that although he was sincere in his efforts, they didn't fit the righteous purpose Jesus had for him. Jesus made Saul see that his efforts were a form of hindrance rather than help.

I can't say what you do in your daily interaction with nouns, but take a very close look at the way you think and react toward people and the things you encounter each day. Your words, facial expression, body gestures and hidden thoughts are either a form of hindrance or help to the program of righteousness. All negatives; holier than thou attitude, judging, hating, superiority; to name a few, are hindrances to God's program. "All positives; loving, kindness, truth, I hurt when you hurt attitude; to name a few, are helpful to God's program. When you do things to hinder the teachings of Jesus you are persecuting Jesus. When you hurt one another, you are hurting Jesus. Look at it this why, if someone hurt your child, especially a loving, obedient child, you feel the same hurt. In other words, hurting your child is hurting you. When you are mean to your spouse, children, friend and people in general, you are being mean to Jesus. Whatever you do to your fellow man you are doing it to Jesus.

Jesus Words are the templates; place them over your thinking and deeds and see if your thinking and deeds fit the templates. In other words, understanding that lying, in any form, is bad. Coveting, jealous, hate, stealing, cheating, adultery, to name as few, are works against righteousness and thus, a hindrance to God's righteous program.

## ONE (YOU) CAN MAKE A DIFFERENCE

John 1:19-23

:19 And this is the record of John, when the Jews sent priests and Levites from Jerusalem to ask him, Who art thou?

:20 And he confessed, and denied not; but confessed, I am not the Christ.

:21 And they asked him, what then? Art thou Elias? And he

saith, I am not. Art thou that prophet? And he answered, No.

:22 Then said they unto him, Who art thou? that we may give an answer to them that sent us. What sayest thou of thyself?

:23 He said, I am the voice of one crying in the wilderness, make straight the way of the Lord, as said the prophet Esaias.

You've heard this before; so have I: "Can one person make a difference? Or, what difference can I make? What is one voice? And he old popular: my one vote won't matter. (This attitude translates into many failures in life.)

The truth is; one individual can make a difference. The lesson in this scripture shows how one-person being obedient to the Word of God can accomplish great things. It shows that as individuals we have a responsibility to carry out the work God has given us to do. But, to do this we must follow the instructions in the bible. God has built the roads and He is not going to rebuild or change the course just because someone doesn't want to follow it. Nor will He accept some road you build because it suits your fancy. You have a talent; you have the ability to do something that is positive and beneficial to human existence on this earth. So, you must use it as given. It is not our goal to prepare someone for heaven. God is the only one to determine who will and won't spend eternal life with him. Our goal is to exercise the talent or ability that God have given us. And I can emphatically say; in exercising that talent we will always show the love and mercy of God. On the flip side, you will learn the punishments for trying to put into God's programs something He said will not be allowed. Don't worry about who is or isn't going to heaven, it's not your job. The Word, not you, will accomplish God's purpose. The most important thing in your life is to obey the Word of God. Who knows; that may be all God is asking you to do. Maybe you can't sing. Maybe you can't teach. Maybe you can't do some of the things you see and hear people doing; so what? You certainly can love. You can be kind, understanding, cooperative, giving and truthful in your interactions with people. We sometimes get so caught up in what others are doing we forget what we can do. Moses, Elijah, Isaiah and other prophets were great men and did great things but their functions were different than John's, but, what they performed, accomplished great things. Paul was a great man in Christ but he was not John and John was not Paul. They both accomplished great things through being obedient to the Word of God.

The scripture shows that many will question your efforts. Many will try to prevent you from carrying out your God given work; that is, exercising what you know is right according to the Word of God and your ability to do it. Jesus continually reminds you that some will go so far as to kill you to prevent you from doing what God has empowered you to do. But again, when exercising your talents let the reality of the Word and your faith in God decide your ultimate decision. If pleasing people is the goal, then you will have failed before you begin; because no matter how many people you may attract to your side; if what you are doing is not in accordance with what God told you to do, then your work is in vain. Listen to what Jesus said about some. "Lord, didn't I cast out devils in your name; and did many good works in you name?" "Depart from me, I don't know you, you workers

215

of iniquity." They were doing something but not what God gave them the talent to do. Look at it this way, you were trained to be an automobile mechanic, but you chose to work as a doctor with no doctor's training. Sure, you may luck up and do something right, but lawfully you are committing a crime. God gave you the talent to sing which would accomplish his purpose through your songs. But, you decided to preach, sure, some might confess God through your preaching, but what was the end results of your preaching? Ignoring what God tells you to do is not being obedient to his word. If all you can do is stay in your house and pray for people, do it with all your heart and might. The prayers of the saints are not lost; God preserve them all.

You have a talent; given to you by God. You are an individual, not a crowd. Take that talent or talents and work it with all your might. Don't look to gather a crowd before you starts; start by yourself. Don't think about what others will or will not say; just exercise your talent with every ounce of strength in you. If you do, your work will accomplish its goal. You have Jesus with you so go ahead, take that step.

## APPRECIATE GOD'S BLESSINGS

Luke 17:12-19

:12 And as he entered into a certain village, there met him ten men that were lepers, which stood afar off:

:13 And they lifted up their voices, and said, Jesus, Master, have mercy on us

:14 And when he saw them, he said unto them, Go shew yourselves unto the priest. And it came to pass, that, as they went, they were cleansed.

:15 And one of them, when he saw that he was healed, turned back and, with a loud voice glorified God.

:16 And fell down on his face at his feet, giving him thanks: and he was a Samaritan.

:17 And Jesus answering said, Were there not ten cleansed? but where are the nine?

:18 There are not found that returned to give glory to God, save this stranger.

:19 And he said unto him, Arise, go thy way: thy faith hath made thee whole.

Jesus is pointing out to us here how easy it is to become unappreciative. The fact that Jesus healed ten lepers and only one returned to thank him for the healing clearly shows the attitudes of the nine that didn't return. We know that during these times the relationship between the Jews and Samaritans were strained, at best. But forget about the general attitudes of people between nations, even communities. Don't try to figure out what nationalities were among the ten. Forget everything but the facts existing between the sick and the healer. The sick wants to be healed of their sickness. In the case of the lepers, their disease was one that banned them from intermingling with society. They knew they were outcasts; they didn't even come close to Jesus. They stood within shouting distance and asked for mercy. Jesus granted their request. But, what happen? Did they become so excited over their healing that they thanked the healer? One did. Looking at the actions of the nine, their attitudes were not one of thankfulness. Let me quickly point out here, this is not judging the nine, but it is looking at their actions and deciding that I will or will not let their actions become a part of my interactions with people. These are the actions and attitudes Jesus want us to see. Note one thing. Jesus didn't bring a railing accusation against the nine, he just pointed out that ten were healed but only one came back to thank God. Ten men received the same blessing but only one really looked at the magnitude of his blessing and realized Jesus had done what their doctors and others claiming healing powers, had not done. They were cured and able to move back into society to enjoy the life of family, friends and all that come with healing. Yet, they didn't stop to thank the one that gave them such a golden opportunity

We, as human beings, ask God in prayer, to fulfill our needs, and give us the things we desire. But, stop and think of your actions and attitudes; are they one of appreciation? Do you really thank Jesus for all the blessings you receive from Him daily? Do you ever stop and look at the fact that no matter how you view it, you are receiving untold blessings from Jesus each day? It is easy to be become like the man praying for long life, but is not thanking Jesus for the breath he's taking at the very moment. We pray for many things but are not being thankful for the things we have at the moment.

The things we pray for are too numerous and varied to mention here; but regardless of what you pray for, be thankful and appreciate what you have already. Look at the magnitude of each heart beat, sight, breath, taste, smell, mobility, roof over your head, transportation, clothing, bread and the list goes on. Where did it all come from? Never think you are the provider. Yes, you may work but where did your strength come from? Where did the knowledge and wisdom needed to do the job come from? I again remind you of the man that told God he could make a man. When God told him to go ahead and make his man, the man stooped down to scoop up dust; but, God stopped him and said: no, make your own dust.

It's very easy to take what God give us and shape it into certain figures and molds and began bragging about what we've done and can do. When we realize the magnitude of each blessing from God and appreciate it enough to give him thanks, we will become humble enough to take our blessing and live in love with our fellow man; the way Jesus wants us to live.

Yes, the lepers followed Jesus' instructions; they headed to see the priest. But they also realized before reaching the priest they were healed. Obedience to God's Word will bring blessings, but what is your attitude after you receive the blessing?

Joseph Haugabrook

## MEASURE YOUR LOVE BY THIS

I Corinthians 10:24

:24 Let no man seek his own, but every man another's wealth.

Listen closely to what this verse is saying. It's saying plainly; when it comes to your daily interaction with people don't do it in a selfish way. When the disciples asked Jesus to teach them to pray, look at what he told them. His example to them did not contain "me" "this" or "I." But rather "us" "give us" "lead us", "deliver us," a very unselfish way of talking to God. Why? Very simple, all of God's responses to our needs and desires are unselfish. Jesus tells us; it is the good will of the Father to give us the kingdom. Can that be called selfish?

Again, when it comes to serving God we do it in the arena of daily interaction with people. And we should be unselfishly willing to share what we have with them. I won't even begin to say what or how much you should share with others. That is always determined by God, who will lay on your heart what and how much to do, when you live in the word and let the word live in you. But, remember, God have blessed you with something; be willing to share it. Please, and don't let your mind get locked in on money while reading this or thinking about your daily actions and deeds among people. I'm not saying don't give money. If you have it, then don't be selfish with it. But I leave how much, and to what cause, to God. God will in his own way, let you know that, when you are obedient to the teachings of Jesus. Mine is not to have you count out dollars and cents for division, or summarize your gains for share giving. Mine is to give you, through Jesus Christ, the spiritual understanding of God's guidance to us for daily living, and, an understanding of how we should interact with people in everything we say and do; our short and long term feelings, emotions and deeds about and toward nouns. It's easy to look at what you have and say; I would give this or that but I might need it later. Or, I would do this or that for that person but I just don't have the time; and many such excuses. Now, I'm not saying that there will never be times when circumstances dictate your delaying giving or helping. But I am saying, even in those times your thoughts and attitudes should be one of sincere desiring to give and help when time and conditions avail themselves.

## LIFE IS NOT FOUND IN EARHLY POSSESSIONS

Luke 12:13-15

:13 And one of the company said unto him, Master, speak to my brother, that he divide the inheritance with me.

:14 And he said unto him, Man, who made me a judge or a divider over you?

:15 And he said unto them, Take heed and beware of covetousness: for a man's life consistent not in the abundance of the things which he possesses.

221

Joseph Haugabrook

Jesus is telling us here what is really important in this life. Look at the conversation between the man and Jesus. The man, by his own words, is saying the things left by their departed love one weren't being shared, but rather taken wholly by his brother. First of all the brother had to be a very selfish person to want everything for himself and not share with his brother, or other siblings as the case may be. Also the brother that came to Jesus had to be thinking hard and serious of finding a way to get what he thought was rightly his because he was a son of the deceased; again, a selfish intent. Bottom line a family was arguing over earthly things and this kind of dispute can lead to some very extreme actions. I have and I'm sure you have too; seen families completely separate, stop speaking even, because of assets left by a departed love one. So, the question becomes, how should situations such as this be handled?

Well, first of all look at what Jesus said to the man that wanted Him to intervene in the dispute. "Man, who made Me a judge or a divider over you?" Your first thought might be, as I'm sure the man's was; Jesus is the judge of us all. And, He will judge righteously. But, Jesus point out very clearly that He is not a judge settling disputes over worldly goods sought after by mankind. If that was the case Jesus would be judging between selfish motives. In other words, since arguing over worldly goods carries a selfish motive, Jesus would be judging which brother was the least or most selfish. And since selfishness is not a part of God's program Jesus is telling us He is not a part of such actions and such actions will be judged at the time of judgment. God gave us free will and He gave us His Word to guide us in exercising that free will; therefore, He expects us to use His Word in

222

handling the events and occurrences in our lives.

Greed, selfishness and the like, are terrible thoughts, thinking and practices. Such things drive people to perform horrific acts against others. I've seen cases where one family member kills another over inheritance. We fight, kill, rob, maim, and worse over things that will soon pass away; things that has no value beyond this world, and does nothing but bring grief when acquired in ways other than what Jesus told us how to acquire them. Read the Old Testament; read the New Testament, God blessed obedient servants with great riches but the riches were acquired by being obedient to God's Word. Earthly things are like putting clothes on a strong healthy body. The clothing can be worn in joy and peace because the body is able to add to the beauty and style of the clothes. The strong straight body makes the clothes fit properly. But, clothes worn on a sick, bent, swollen, and aching body will not add one thing to the style or beauty, it will, in reality, take away from what could be beautiful and stylish. Gaining earthly things by being obedient to God's Word will let us know how to appreciate and fit such gains into our lives making our lives beautiful. Things that Jesus tells us will pass away will never be worth fighting over or gained by lying, cheating, robbing, killing and the likes. Seek, you first the kingdom of God and all these things will be added to you. In other words, work each day to be obedient to God's Word and the promises of God will be given to you. Ask Jesus how to approach situations arising in your life; not get involved in arguments; especially when it's going to lead to you getting your way, whether someone else like it or not.

## FIRST, UNDERSTND YOURSELF

Romans 12:1-2

:1 beseech you therefore, brethren, by the mercies of God, that ye present your bodies a living sacrifice, holy, acceptable unto God, which is your reasonable service.

:2 And be not conformed to this world: but be ye transformed by the renewing of your mind, that ye may prove what is that good and acceptable, and perfect, will of God.

(Read the entire 12th chapter) Verse 21 gives a summation of the thought in chapter 12)

In verse one; present your body a living sacrifice, holy, acceptable to God; is what God expects of us all; our question may be; how do I get there? The answer is found in verse two; and be not conformed to this world, but be ye transformed by the renewing of your mind. If you are wondering what transforming the mind is; think of your normal tendency of actions and reactions to what are said and done to you. Ask yourself, and answer honestly; what is my response when someone curses me, or hit me or do things I don't like? What is my response when I feel I've been treated wrong, cheated or called a degrading name or some other negative action against me? If your answer is in the negative, for whatever reason, that is, curse back, hit back, seek revenge etc; then you need to change your thinking to the point you can act or react in the positive. That is; be kind, loving, helpful, caring, cooperative, and all the positives that embodies love. Yes, you may be called a coward, chicken, weak, and worse; so what, when you learn the word of God you know who you are and that what others call you doesn't make you become what they say you are.

It is very easy to be transformed by the world. It's done quite often without being realized. In other words, when you react negatively because of what people say or do; the conditions you face or the things you see, you are letting it shape your thinking and actions and thus transforming your response to that of the world, or, doing Satan's bidding. God is saying to us; when you find yourself thinking and acting in this manner, compare it to the guidance I've given you and make the necessary adjustments. Remember, we all have the power, given by God, to control our thinking and actions. Don't hate because someone else hate. Don't do wrong because it's the popular thing to do. Don't do something just to please others. Don't act or react because it's the right thing to do in man's perceptions. We make our body a living sacrifice to God by being loving toward our fellow man, trusting and believing in God. You can't help but be holy when you let your actions and reactions be dictated by the guidance God has given to all; and not by the dictates of man.

Verse three tells us not to think of ourselves more highly than we should. If your question is: how high is that? Well, I won't cite any particular scripture because the whole bible tell how God feels about us beginning in Genesis, in the manner in which he made us; but for reference look at Revelation 5:10. God think highly of us and want us to think highly of ourselves. Not bragging, or being holier than thou, but proudly living a life where you look to God for answers to any condition you face; that is, you hold your head up and smile, knowing through faith and love the God that created and control all things have your best interest at heart and will make all things right in your life.

When you can be positive, not worrying or fearing conditions around you, loving without exceptions, willing to help anyone, even those who hate you, you can safely say you understand the thought given in verse 21 and are fulfilling it.

## SHOULD WE BE CONCERNED ABOUT THE END OF THE WORLD?

Luke 21:29-33

:29 And he spake to them a parable: behold the fig tree, and all the trees;

:30 When they now shoot forth, ye see and know of your own selves that summer is now at hand.

:31 So likewise ye, whey ye see these things come to pass, know ye that the kingdom of God is nigh at hand.

:32 Verily I say unto you, This generation shall not pass away, till all be fulfilled.

:33 Heaven and earth shall pass away; but my words shall not pass away.

Jesus is very plain on this topic. He explained the things that will take place prior, and right up to the end. Then, in the verses listed above he gave meaning to the things we will see taking place. He very clearly and factual compared the two events; the budding of the fig tree and the events happening in the earth. Jesus said in the ninth verse; But when ye shall hear of wars and commotions, be not terrified for these things must first come to pass; but the end is not by and by.

Jesus is telling us that when we see these things happening in many different places, especially in places where they normally wouldn't happen, or have never happen before, then compare it to the fig tree, and other trees. You know that budding of the trees signal the coming of summer when the process of its function on earth will reach maturity. The hot weather may not be upon you at the time you see the buds but you have no doubt that it's coming in a short while. So, with all the things we see happening in the world today, especially floods, famine and such; in places where they ought not be happening, or have never happen before, you know for certain that the end is not far away. Jesus said the generation in which all these things occur; that is, seeing them happening at the same time or one right after the other in many different places, that generation will not pass till the ending of time is fulfilled. With the budding of the trees, that year will not pass before summer and the tree fulfilling its function is fulfilled. Today we see a lot happening; so, read, watch, pray, and be patience, as Jesus told us in verse 19, and let Jesus speak to our hearts; guiding us in everything we do.

One thing; the end is coming and we will be a part of it, whether we are alive or not. Also our greatest concern now is; making certain that when we face death, our soul will have been prepared to spend eternity with Jesus. The end is not something to worry or be fearful about; living in this life according to the words of Jesus Christ is our greatest concern. We have our time on earth to get it right, it is our main concern, and should be our goal.

## LOOK CLOSELY AT YOUR REASONS FOR SEEKING JESUS

John 6:26-29

:26 Jesus answered them and said, Verily, verily I say unto you, ye seek me, not because ye saw the miracles, but because ye did eat of the loaves, and were filled.
:27 Labour not for the meat which perisheth, but for that meat which endureth unto everlasting life, which the son of man shall give unto you; for him hath God the Gather sealed.

:28 Then said they unto him, what shall we do, that we might work the works of God?

:29 Jesus answered and said unto them, This is the work of God, that ye believe on him whom he hath sent.

When I read what Jesus is saying here, I can't help but look at the world around me and the reasons so many people are seeking to use Jesus name in their daily functions. They are doing exactly what Jesus told the people they were doing; seeking him, not for a spiritual reason, but to fulfill a carnal desire.

I am not condemning any minister, nor do I want to give that appearance. But, I am stating a fact, and, I might add, a common practice in many congregations today. That fact is: serving God has become synonymous with fund raising. The success of church programs are measured by the amount of money raised. The success of annual; or some other frequency; revivals, are not measured by the number of souls revived or brought to God, but rather by the amount of money raised during that period. The greatest worker for God in the church is the one that causes the most money to flow into the treasury. Clearly, many today are holding up the name of Jesus before them to gain a carnal desire, and ignoring he fact that doing exactly what Jesus says to do will manifest his promises in this life and the life to come.

People are being told that working for God means being in church every Sunday, supporting church programs financially, because if they can't be there in person send or leave money for the collection. Which, again, means a fund raiser, no matter the name attached to it? They are told as long as they support the church programs God will fulfill all their needs. Of course very clever words are used in saying it. Again, this is not to condemn, but to look at what is being taught and practiced. Is this what Jesus said should be done? If the programs are designed to give an understanding of how you should conduct your life each day to improve your relationship with Jesus, then yes, supporting it will manifest the promises of Jesus in your life. You know better than I, what you hear each Sunday in your congregation, but, and if, it's not what the word of God says no matter who says it, you are not going to receive the benefits God promised. You can't fool God; talk about a mind reader, He knows what you will think before you think it. Let me say again, and I emphasis this; all the beauty, comfort, and enjoyment are contained in the program of God. But it is an indivisible part of eternal life; and, you can't reach it or have it without gaining or accepting eternal life, and you can't have eternal life without being obedient to the word of God, and you can't be obedient without understanding what the word say do. When God gave Noah instructions to build the ark he had to follow the instructions to the letter. There was no room for Noah's input. God knew what it would take for the ark to withstand what it had to go through and save its occupants. There is no room for our input into God's program. He knows what we need to do in order to obtain eternal life and enjoy the things he has provided for our enjoyment in this life. And we must do what Noah and other great men of God did, follow his instructions to the letter. Don't seek him just for the things that will vanish after this life is over; but rather those things that will insure eternal life and enjoyment in this life.

I don't know your reason for wanting to be a part of God's program. But, it should not be to fulfill some desire for worldly things. Jesus told the crowd that was looking for Him, not to come to Him for things that will someday vanish. Come for things that are eternal. Jesus is trying very hard to tell us that if we put things in the proper order, everything else will fall in place. If we come to Him seeking help to be kind, loving, sharing, cooperative, understanding, increasing our faith, obedient to His Word and other positives things, then other things we need and desire, such as money to pay bills and help others, homes, automobiles, and the list goes on, is already a part of the program. It is the only program whereby you can have your cake and eat it too. You can believe in Jesus Christ, which mean you will have faith, trust, and be obedient to His Word, and have all the luxuries of this life.

Take a good look at what you do daily and how you do it; compare it to instructions in the bible; if they don't match, try adjusting what you are doing because the instructions in the bible are right, and will not change to your ways; you must do the changing.

## HOW DO WE KNOW WE ARE WALKING IN DARKNESS

I John 1:5-8

:5 This then is the message which we have heard of him, and declare unto you, that God is light, and in him is no darkness at all.

:6 If we say that we have fellowship with him and walk in darkness, we lie, and do not the truth:

:7 But if we walk in the light, as he is in the light, we have fellowship one with another, and the blood of Jesus Christ, his son cleanseth us from all sin.

:8 If we say that we have no sin, we deceive ourselves and the truth is not in us.

Just how do we know we are walking in darkness?

The 5th verse tells us plainly that God is light and there is no darkness in Him at all. So, if we are walking with Him, or have fellowship with Him we are not in darkness, otherwise we are just lying to ourselves, So, think about this, examine yourself, and see if you are walking in the light or darkness.

First we see that the light is truth; the Word of God, which is truth; If we live by the Word of God, obey his commandments, and follow the examples set down by Jesus Christ, His Son, then we are walking in the light.

So, it's plain to see that if we are not living by the Word of God, obeying His commandments and following the examples set by Jesus, then we are walking in darkness. In darkness we do not have fellowship with Him no matter what we tell ourselves. I want to point out one important thing here. Going to church, no matter the denomination or religion, does not in itself put you in the light. You can attend church each time the doors open and still be walking in darkness. What put you in the light are the examples set down by Jesus Christ. Therefore you must know the Word. You can't build something you have no idea of what it's suppose to be, without clear instruction. The only way you will know what God requires of you is to understand his Word. If you don't understand God's Word how can you do it? How can you say you are obeying His commandments if you don't know what they are? I had a carpenter building a house for me and although he could read blueprints there was one part of a complex roof that he got completely wrong because he just didn't understand what was suppose to be done. He thought he was right, even argued that he was until he was shown by a person who understood the blueprints and showed him where he was wrong. Jesus has made things perfectly clear, plus He has sent men and women into the world to clarify His Word to those who don't understand it. One simple way to check whether you are walking in the light is look at your attitude toward love. If you fine that you love people in general without exception; that is, want the very best for them; good homes, loving marriages, obedient children, all the comforts and conveniences of life; plus being obedient to God's Word then you are in the light. If you find your self falling short in this area, it's a good sign you are walking in darkness. You see, in these times, the cart has been put ahead of the horse. Men are seeking to understand man, rather than the Word of God. Seek to understand the Word of God and the understanding of man will become clear. You can't use confusion to clarify confusion; just as you can't use a lie to arrive at the truth. Don't expect to use sand to build a solid foundation. In Washington, D.C. where a great portion of the land on which the city set are land fill; bottles, cans, and other debris mixed with dirt. Builders drove large, tall steel beams beyond the fill into the solid part of the ground in order to put buildings on solid foundations. The world is like the land under DC. It takes knowing the truth and understanding God's Word to establish fellowship with Him and stay in the light. If you find yourself hating another human being, not working to make things better for all humanity, stop and check your position, you may have stepped into darkness.

Joseph Haugabrook

## ACCEPTING RESPONSIBILITY FOR OUR ACTS

Genesis 3:12

:12 And the man said, the woman whom thou gavest to be with me, she gave me of the tree and I did eat.

This is straight forward and to the point; accepting responsibility instead of pointing the finger. This is one of the earliest examples of man's shortcoming and it still exist today; man wanting to separate himself from his own acts when he's caught in violation of any rule, law, or promise. It's the ole "the devil made me do it excuse. God gave Adam specific instruction of what he could and could not eat; and the reason why. When Adam violated God's instructions, or commandment, and God called him on the carpet for it; Adam immediately tried to distance himself from his own act. Look at what Adam, in reality, said; Oh no! It's not my fault, the woman You gave me, it's her fault. She gave me of the tree otherwise I wouldn't have eaten from it. First, he blames Eve, and then he blames God. She and You are the reason I ate of the tree.

But, let's not judge Adam. We today, have the same opportunity to obey Jesus Christ as Adam had to obey God. Eve didn't beat Adam down and force the fruit down his throat; Adam ate of his own freewill. Yes, Eve offered it to him but he didn't have to eat it. Eve was deceived by the devil and passed that deception on to Adam and Adam accepted it knowing full well that It was in violation of God's commandment. The devil was, and still is, angry with God for being kicked out of Heaven and wants to destroy His creation; starting with Adam and Eve. And the same deception he used on Eve, then Adam, is still being practiced today; find the weakest spot and exploit it.

That process is alive and well right now. It can come in the form of another person doing something and getting another person involved. It can be on television radio or the news paper. It can be on a movie screen or just hearing someone talking. Motivated by greed, a company will use all kind of tricks and deceptions to get the public to buy its product. Motivated by lust, even ministers will use deceptions to commit adultery with a female; even young teens. But you get the picture! Satan initiate the deed in the form of a thought and man carry it out it the form of physical actions, then, when the deed becomes known tries to distance himself from it.

The acts of distancing oneself from his actions are the reasons for the troubles and ills of the world. The fact that man wants to hold himself up as right, pure and undefiled cause's problem in the family, the community and nation. The husband says he's right. The wife says she's right. The children say they are right. This thinking and attitude starting in the home; spills over into the neighborhood and affect every segment of the state and nation. A wrong is committed and the one committing the wrong tries to separate himself from it by lying or pointing the finger. It's the blacks fault; it's the Whites fault; it's the Hispanics fault; it's the Chinese's fault; it's the Japanese's fault; it's the fast foods fault; and the list goes on. Nations are fighting nations because no one nation will accept the responsibility for its own acts. When people, including nations, start accepting their own weaknesses and stop trying to be perfect, pure and undefiled, then they will be able to see what their pretense of righteousness and strength are doing to everybody else. How can a liar go around accusing someone else of lying? They are both guilty? The same holds true for every act that violates God's commandments.

The practice of blaming others for our own deeds is a great weakness in mankind, and it will become a part of our thinking and practices if you let it. Stay with the Word of God; be obedient and don't be deceived by someone or something telling you something different from what it says.


## DON'T LET ANYONE OR ANYTHING STOP YOU

Matthew 20:29-34

:29 And as they departed from Jericho, a great multitude followed him

:30 And, behold, two blind men sitting by the way side; when they heard that Jesus passed by, cried out, saying, Have mercy on us, O Lord, thou son of David.

:31 And the multitude rebuked them, because they should hold their peace: but they cried the more, saying, Have mercy on us, O Lord, thou son of David.

:32 And Jesus stood still, and called them, and said, What will ye that I shall do unto you?

:33 They say unto him, Lord, that our eyes may be opened.

:34 So Jesus had compassion on them, and touched their eyes: and immediately their eyes received sight, and they followed him.

This is a powerful lesson on self determination. First, look at the words "great multitude" "multitude warned" "be quiet." Second, look at the phrase, "but they cried out all the more." Now, consider the individuals. These were two blind men, learning at that time, that Jesus was passing their way. They had not seen Jesus perform miracles because they were blind. But, they had heard about Him and believed. Their minds and determination were not focused on customs, nor the high priests and his followers, just what they believed about Jesus.

These were determined to get Jesus attention. There is no doubt more than one person in that large group of people, tried to make the blind men, shut up. The blind men were warned. In other words the demand to shut up was strongly issued. These blind men couldn't see those issuing the demands; whether they were big, strong, mean or otherwise. But, to them, it made no difference. They were determined to hear from Jesus; to talk with Him; to ask their desire of Him.

God, has through Jesus given us his perfect Word. You may not always understand. There may be some who don't understand at all; meaning you may be blind to the facts some or all of the time. But, depending on your determination you can get the truth, and all that goes with it. You must make up your mind that the bible is the Word of

God and you are going to stick with its teachings. These blind men knew God, through the Law and the Prophets. And what they were told through the prophets had become reality.

Because of not understanding the Word of God, some don't see all the miracles being performed each day. And, because so many have gotten use to only believing what they see, smell and touch, Jesus is pushed out of their daily functions. It is these, the one that are not practicing the teaching of Jesus, that will try to discourage you from studying and practicing the teaching of Jesus.

Yes, it's true; it's reality, you will be discouraged from practicing the teachings of Jesus in your daily interactions with nouns. You will see and hear all kind of negative things about the Word of God. There will be many, so called, legal reasons for you not to use or practice the Word of God. And yes some may seek to persecute you in the courts. In short, you may be pressured or threatened to keep quiet about Jesus. But, what is your stance? Are you going to let the multitude (majority) decide whether you should believe Jesus and practice it openly in your dealings? Are you going to let "Politically correct" become your practice? Or, are you going to let the Word of God be your guide? The Bible is our instructions for living; these instructions come from God. It's up to you to believe and use them. It just depends on how determine you are.

Let's Talk About Jesus

## THE GREAT INVITATION

Matthew 11:28-30

:28 Come unto me all ye that labour and are heavy laden, and I will give you rest.

:29 Take my yoke upon you, and learn of me; for I am meek and lowly in heart: and ye shall find rest unto your souls.

:30 For my yoke is easy, and my burden is light.

This is great for those seeking the love of Jesus, peace in their lives, and an understanding of how to successfully conduct their daily lives.

As you battle with the occurrences of daily life, you sometimes find yourself feeling like throwing up your hands in disgust. You may even say "it's not worth it!" and quit, even if temporary. I've seen some so frustrated with finance, mates, children, work and other problems that they talk seriously about just disappearing and getting away from it all; some do.

Life is full of things that weary the spirit; sickness, bills, special needs for a mate or children, automobile problems, lack of finance, and the list goes on. You try and nothing seems to work. Sometimes it seems your prayers are not being answered. You feel, I just can't go on, I'm too tired and weak I just can't carry this burden. Well, Jesus is saying he understand the burden you are carrying. He understands the fight you are waging. He wants you to come to Him with whatever you are carrying, give it to Him and get rid of worrying, pressure, the spirit of defeat, and the feeling of being alone with no one caring.

Jesus is asking you to come to Him and let Him show you the way to peace and rest. He is not saying, there won't be problems, He is saying He will show you the solution to those problems. He will provide whatever is needed to solve the problems that confront you in this life. And, eternal life after this life is over.

During the celebration of Jesus death and resurrection, think about the love He had for us all in going to the cross. And add to it the great invitation He gave to all people. In this life you are bound to encounter problems, but isn't it comforting to know there is a way out of them all? As the song says; Come to Jesus.

## MUSTARD SEED FAITH

Matthew 17:19-21

:19  Then came the disciples to Jesus apart, and said, Why could not we cast him out?

:20  And Jesus said unto them, Because of your unbelief: for verily I say unto you, if ye have faith as a grain of mustard seed, ye shall say unto this mountain, remove hence to yonder place; and it shall remove; and nothing shall be impossible unto you.

:21   Howbeit this kind goeth not out but by prayer and fasting.

Take a look at what Jesus is saying about faith in God. Forget the size of the mustard seed. Forget that it is a food, medicine, can soothe irritations and more. Look at how Jesus uses it to show faith and the power of faith.

When we consider the little seed itself we see a very durable little fellow. The little seed will sprout and grow in almost any condition. It will adapt to many different, or changing conditions. It is, in reality, tough, durable and determined. Yet, there are a few conditions that it needs help; but for the most part it stands on its own.

In the case of the Disciples not being able to cast out the demon from the child, they needed, as Jesus stated, something else added. The Disciples needed enough faith not to doubt, and, in this instant, needed to fast and pray. This is an excellent example of why Christians should fast and pray often, because tough problems can pop up at any time. And as the old saying goes; always be prepared.

Jesus is saying that faith will work on all kind of problems when individuals don't let the conditions facing them make them doubt. The mustard seed don't care whether it's thrown on stony ground, shallow soil, deep soil, dry soil or any areas not conducive for it to sprout and grow. If planted, it will grow. It's the same as the little seed saying; I don't care how rough it is, I'm going to sprout, grow and produce my fruit. Yes, you can face some tough problem;

conditions that seems overwhelming. But, Jesus is saying; the solution to the problem is faith. Sometimes it may require a little more; it may require fasting and praying, but never lose faith. Use faith always, you may have to add fasting and prayer, but never lose faith.

You may be facing some tough decision right now, you may have a problem that seems to large to solve; my advice is think about the mustard seed; not about the size but rather it's determination to be what it was created to be. If it didn't push aside conditions and grow, someone would miss out on its food, medicines made from it, the protection it provides for birds and the shade it produces for many to enjoy. When we let conditions, and problems stop us many people can suffer because of it. Losing faith is like salt losing its savor. So, no matter how hard it seem, no matter how difficult it gets, no matter what is said about you or what attempts are made to stop you, keep believing in Jesus; that he is leading you out of the condition in which you find yourself. In other words, hold on to your faith.

## POWER OF THE TONGUE

James 3:7-10

:7   For every kind of beasts, and of birds, and of serpents, and of things in the sea, is tamed, and hath been tamed of mankind:

:8    But the tongue can no man tame; it is an unruly evil, full of deadly poison.

:9    Therewith bless we God, even the Father; and herewith curse we men, which are made after the similitude of God.

:10    Out of the same mouth proceedeth blessing and cursing. My brethren, these things ought not so to be.

We wake, go through our day and back to sleep again, with threats and raving of wars and destructions among human beings. Yes, the words "Peace and Protection are thrown in, to divert the real reasons behind the raving, which are; wars and fights emanating from the lusts, whether for power or other things within the members of mankind.

Think about the causes of these fights and hurts among us. Think how one little word, uttered by the tongue can cause the death or destruction of another individual or nation. Think how one little word can break up a marriage; separate family members; throw a community into disarray, or causes nations to go to war.

When I was a small boy I saw a very nasty fight between two older boys because one boy drew a line in the dirt and told the other boy, "I dare you to cross it." Six little words tore clothing, bruised faces and other parts of the body and got both boys in trouble with their parents. The whole silly thing started over who was the strongest.

Think about the things families and nations are fighting over today. It all boils down to self centered, self seeking aims. One person wants to be thought of as, most beautiful, most handsome, most popular, best dressed, richer, smarter, healthier, have more luxuries, and the list goes on. Nations want to be thought of as most powerful, more progressive, has the largest army, and the list goes on. The things that matters are clearly pushed aside. Love, understanding, cooperation, and positive communication are looked on as weaknesses that should be avoided. The tongue is the vehicle by which the thoughts of men are made known. It is a powerful tool for love and peace. It is a very destructive, yet powerful tool for wars among us, whether in the home, community or nation. All of our wars start with words of men. And with all the wars fought over the centuries, none has really brought peace. For while the fighting and killing may stop for a while; plans for war still go on.

These are times we should be using our tongue to bless, to speak truth, to show love, understanding and cooperation. Today, nations have drawn a line in the sand and are daring other nations to cross it; and families seem to be following suit. God gave us this powerful tool to bring joy and peace to ourselves and to others. But, it cannot bring war and peace at the same time; so you have to choose which one yours will bring. Whatever your determination is, let it bring joy, peace, love and hope to all people.

Let's Talk About Jesus

## RESISTING TEMPTATION

Luke 4:3-4

:3 And the devil said unto him, if thou be the son of God, command this stone that it be made bread.
:4 And Jesus answered him, saying It is written, that man shall not live by bread alone, but by every word of God.

It's important for everyone to be ever vigilant because the devil is always waiting for the right time to spring his lies on you.

Lets be clear on this; the devil knew from the outset that he would not fool Jesus to accept his lies. The devil was well aware that Jesus knew all about him, and he certainly knew that Jesus was the Son of God. So, why did all this happen? It is the ultimate example of the length the devil will go to make your interactions with people be in violation of God's Word. Thus, it happened for our sakes, that we will know the tricks of the devil and his persistence in getting mankind involved in them.

Only the first trick the devil presented to Jesus will be discussed here. It is the one that touched a personal need of Jesus at the time. Jesus had just completed a forth day fast, and, He was hungry. You must remember, Jesus was in the flesh; requiring all the needs of a fleshy being. So, Jesus was hungry; and as well you know hunger can cause a person to do things out of the ordinary to get food; Jacob and Esau is a prime example. Hunger has driven people to steal, rob, kill and worse. Many have gone to great length to satisfy their hunger; Jesus was hungry, a need that the flesh seeks to satisfy. So in come the devil with the solution; "hey, go on, you need to eat, turn this stone to bread."

Note the prime motivator in the devil's effort. "If you are the Son of God. The devil hit Jesus with the very thing that fleshy being are most venerable to; a challenge to prove you are what you say you are. How many people have been murdered, raped, maimed, and worse because someone dared them to prove their word? You say you are this, or that, now prove it! You get the picture.

The devil will never try to enter your life through your strong points; he will always hit your weakest areas at the most opportune time; when you are at your weakest or lowest point spiritually. Make no mistake, the devil and his imps are watching you twenty four seven and are patience enough to wait until the best moment to spring on you. A moment when, for some reason, you are angry at your mate, children, coworker, employer, your car broke down, you stubbed your toe, cut your finger, slipped on ice, no money for rent or bills and the list goes on. The devil to the rescue; Hey, I have the perfect answer; knock his or her block off, steal that, rob him, get even, cuss the bill collector out; you are a man, or you are a woman, you don't need to take that, everybody else is doing it, and the list goes on.

Remember, the devil is in the background no matter where you are or what you are doing. In all of your daily interactions with nouns he is watching; ready to spring in with a word or deed as you seek to deal with the situations of life.

How can you keep him out of your acts and deeds?

Or, out of your business? The only way is: knowing the teachings of God and following them to the letter; because God acts on his exact word.

## DON'T ASK; WHY ME GOD? SAY, HELP ME GOD

Read the first three chapters of Daniel

The story of Daniel, Shadrach, Meshach, and Abednego give a very special message on why we should never ask "Why me God?" but rather, ask for God's help in the situation you find yourself. From the beginning of the book of Daniel, we find these four servants of God in extreme situations. First, they were captives (slaves). Second, they were put in situations that required them to compromise their faith, devotion and service to God. They were demanded to eat what the King had set aside for them. But, by not wavering in their faith they got around that demand. Third, they had to come up with knowing what the king had dreamed and interpreting the dream; God gave them the answer to that problem, which spared their lives and the lives of many more. Next, they were asked to worship an idol that the king had set up for all his people to worship. Again, they did not compromise their faith; they held fast and" God freed them from the death penalty placed on them by the king. These first three chapters of Daniel show us plainly why we should never question where we are, when we got there, or why we are there. When we find ourselves in a situation, no matter how mild or extreme, ask God to help you out of if and let Him perform it in His manner.

In today's society many find themselves in many situations to include; financial problems, physical and mental sickness, marital problems, children problems and family problems in general. Some find themselves in trouble with drugs, alcohol, cheating, lying, stealing, killing, robbing envy and the list goes on. But, once in the condition, don't point fingers, don't try to assign blame, not even to self, just look at what you are being faced with and realize that it is a problem, and ask God to help you overcome it. Ask God to give you the solution to the problem; then accept and do what God tells you to do. There is no doubt about it, God will honor his word; he will keep his promise, if we do what he asked us to do.

God has given his Holy Word; a promise he will fulfill if we follow the teachings outlined in his bible. But we can't be doubtful or afraid to practice it in our everyday interaction with nouns. Daniel didn't stop praying because he was threatened with being put in a den of hungry lions. The three Hebrews boys didn't compromise their faith in God because they were threatened with being thrown in a fiery furnace. Problems sometimes push us to the point of trying something other than trusting and depending on God. The promise of a quick easy solution sometimes seems a better way than faith, trust and patience. "But, if you be patience and don't lose faith, God will work it out in a manner that not only benefit you but many more. Look at how their faith changed the king and many more that seen what happen in the lion's den and the fiery furnace. We never know what situation we will find ourselves in but we should never forget that God is always in control and what we see as bad could very well be a great blessing to self and many more people.

## LOVING YOUR CHILD TO DEATH

Deuteronomy 5:16
Matthew 15:4-6

:Deutronomy15 4-6
:5:16  Honour thy father and thy mother, as the Lord thy God hath commanded thee; that thy days may be prolonged, and that it may go well with thee, in the land which the Lord thy God giveth thee.
Matthew 15:4-6
:4  For God commanded, saying, Honour thy father and mother: and, He that curseth father or mother, let him die the death.

:5  But ye say, Whosoever shall say to his father or his mother, it is a gift, by whatsoever thou mightest be profited by me;

:6  And honour not his father or his mother, he shall be free. Thus have ye made the commandment of God of none effect by your tradition.

Never, in modern times have the above scriptures been more relevant than now. The common saying in my young years was: "Children bury the parents, not parents the children. Today that saying has taken a one hundred and eighty degree turn. Although there is no written law, spiritually or otherwise; that children will bury parents; it is in keeping with the commandment of God; "honour thy father and mother that thy days may be prolonged, and it may go well with thee."

You see here that Moses, in the beginning of God's people Israel as a nation, impressed upon them temperance in following the commandments of God; because God's commandments are unchangeable and will apply to everyone without exception.

In Matthew chapter15, Jesus warned the people again of breaking the same commandment. Notice, and please let it sink in, the thing that God commanded Moses, and Jesus didn't change it. Children must honor their father and mother or die the death. Just because the traditions of men say otherwise, does not change the original commandment of God. God's punishment for dishonoring parents is a shortening of days on this earth. Letting your kids become disrespectful to you in the name of love, or following the trends of the times, are, plain and simple, loving them to death. The way to guarantee a short life for your child is to let them be disrespectful, and sassy. I cannot over emphasis the importance of rearing your child beginning at an early age, to respect mother and father. Note: it doesn't matter whether the mother is fulfilling all motherly duties, or the father fulfilling all fatherly duties, the child is to respect them regardless of their actions. No excuses are given for the child to dishonor, or disrespect their parents. God will deal with the mother or father that fails to fulfill their responsibilities. No one in the family group is exempt from God's commandment to the family. Mothers and fathers must raise a child in the way he ought to go. That is in a manner that will fulfill the commandments of God. That responsibility is given by God to the man and woman responsible for the birth of the child. Am I saying that adoption is contrary to the word of God? God forbid. Adoption is a very good thing, because some are parents from being obedient to the commandments of God. Parents by the commandments of God are held liable for the child born to them.

Let's fast forward to present day societies. Parents, in what is viewed as modern times are strictly controlled and severely hampered in rearing their own children. Ineffective agencies created and perpetuated by government mainly as an election tool, which have led to greed and worse, have taken child control out of parent's hands. Children can, as some will, be disrespectful, hateful and worse with the blessing of the law. Of course I don't have to cite the many ways children are controlling parents instead of the other way around, with the parents helpless to do anything about it. But, is parent's ability to control conditions in the home lessened? Better yet; do modern thinking, practices, and laws, preempt the commandments of God? No, and a thousand times no; restraints put on parents today, came as a result of parents neglecting, at an early age, to properly train their children, then, telling and letting politicians formulate laws to do what they say they couldn't do. So, if parents are responsible for the restrictive laws being on the books, parents can change them.

Parents are responsible for teaching their children,

beginning at an early age to be respectful to parents and others. God makes no allowances for modern interpretations of his commandments. Man is to follow the instructions as given in the bible.

## WHAT ARE CHILDISH THINGS?

I Corinthians 13:11

:13 When I was a child, I spake as a child, I understood as a child, I thought as a child; but when I became a man, I put a way childish things.

There is one thing that is easy to forge; even with Christians. We tend to let the idea that; what I'm doing is better or greater than what some other person is doing because of the guiding factor in our lives. We can easily forget that the bottom line in our relationship with God is: love and obedience. And it doesn't matter whether we are male or female, old or young, or what our names are; loving God and obeying His Word is the goal, and will receive the same fullness of the promised blessings. Don't try to decide who is more important; the one planting the corn, the one fertilizing it; or the one keeping the weeds out. The goal is, good ears of corn, and all three are working to produce it. So, look closely at what the verses are saying to us: "when I was a child;" "when I became a man." Let's bring "when I was a child" closer to home and think about your childhood. You were probably, like most youth; pranksters, teasers, and more. You did a lot of things that, at the time, you thought was funny. Of course, sometimes you did things designed to hurt others; like called them names talked about their looks, clothing, family conditions, or ability to learn. In short you did many things because you didn't fully understand what neither the short or long term effects were on the receiver of you acts. You spoke, carried out acts or did things out of character for good taste, human decency and respect. And yes, it's called childish because it is a way of excusing an act of misunderstanding. We normally rationalize, that he or she is a child and don't know any better. What we are saying is they are not responsible for their act because they are too young to have known better. Also, children seem to try and fit most interactions into a game format; it is their way of keeping it interesting. And, rightly so, youth have not lived long enough to experience the seriousness of negative interactions with nouns. Therefore seeing only the fun side of life, they try to make everything they do as fun, more important than their interacting with others. This many times, carry over into adulthood.

When I became a man: adds the other side of life; wisdom and knowledge of the consequences of words and actions. Example: I yelled at my employee and lost an excellent worker because he or she quit. I yelled at my employer and lost a very good job because he or she fired me. I got a speeding ticket, because I was doing eighty in a fifty mile zone. When I was fourteen, I had a friend that was sixteen and driving. He loved driving fast and taking sharp curves at high speed. To him it was fun to see how fast he could take a curve without flipping the car. He gave no thought to the outcome of rolling the car. His fast driving

253

caused him to hit two cars at the same time totaling one and seriously damaging his and the other one. He was blessed to only have minor scrapes; he and the other drivers. His fast driving with no thoughts of consequences was childish.

"I put away childish things." I realized my words and actions can negatively affect others. I can cause someone to commit adultery, lie, steal, kill, use drugs, drink alcohol, give up without trying, become homeless, and much more just by refusing to accept truth and facts that are before me daily. I realize that I let the wisdom and knowledge, learned through truth and facts, dictate my interaction with nouns. Paul killed Christians until he learned the evil of his actions. We obey the word of God because we gain wisdom and knowledge of the purpose of his teaching. Truth and facts demonstrate to us that you don't have to kill, lie, cheat, rob, deceive, and generally commit sin, to have your wants and needs met in this world.

Acting without having wisdom and knowledge is, plain and simple; childish. Letting the truth of God's Word dictate your action is, plain and simple, becoming a man. And the only way to do that is to study, and pray to God for an understanding of His Word so that you can apply it in all your interactions with nouns.

## BEING UNEQUALLY YOKED WITH UNBELIEVERS

2 Corinthians 6:14-18

:14 Be ye not unequally yoked together with unbelievers: for what fellowship hath righteousness with unrighteousness? And what communion hath light with darkness?

:15 And what concord hath Christ with Belial? Or what part hath he that believeth with an infidel?

:16 And what agreement hath the temple of God with idols? For ye are the temple of the living God; as God hath said, I will dwell in them and walk in them; and I will be their God, and they shall be my people.

:17 Wherefore come out from among them and be ye separate saith the Lord, and touch not the unclean thing; and I will receive you,
:18 And will be a Father unto you, and ye shall be my sons and daughters, saith the Lord almighty.

Paul, through the mercies and knowledge of Jesus, pointed out something very important in our interaction with people. But first, let me clear up something that, for many years I was confused about due to the way I received it from others. Do not be unequally yoked with unbelievers; meant to me, a husband being married to an unbelieving wife; or a wife being married to an unbelieving husband, and, I accepted it as such. However, to make a long story short, I had only a vague understanding of this scripture, which meant I believed and practiced marriage as a yoke, connecting a man and woman and that yoke was nothing more than a strong desire to complete some act of satisfaction I had conceived.

First and foremost, marriage is not a yoke. God explained that at the outset of this union between man and woman. There was nothing about the two being harnessed together. God made it clear that the man and woman shall become one flesh. Which means each one wants the very best for the other. Their interactions; thinking, planning, rearing their family, keeping the bonds of marriage free of outside interference and making the family a loving, caring, understanding and cooperative unit is done on an agreeable basis. No arguing, fighting, harsh words, selfishness and finger pointing; just a close, loving unit that, in their interaction with each other, can't be distinguished as anything but one. A believing wife could be the one to save the unbelieving husbandly; or the believing husband could be the one to save the unbelieving wife.

So, this scripture is not referring to marriage. It is, however, speaking about becoming involved with unbelievers in the general population. During the time I was in business I met a gentleman that told me about an incident he got involved in. He needed money to produce a product he felt sure would be a hit with consumers. The bank wouldn't loan him the money he needed so he finally got the money from a loan shark. As a result; he was compelled to do things against his integrity before he was finally rid of the loan shark. There are many cases where a person has compromised his or her position because of getting involved with someone in a personal or business matter. I've seen and heard; and I'm sure you have too where church leaders and members becoming involved in shady money making schemes. Leaders becoming involved knowing at the outset the act is wrong and against the teachings of Jesus Christ, but, they want to gain some earthly asset. There are so many way to become yoked with evil it is impossible to list them all here; but what the scripture is telling us is don't let our self get hooked up with people doing things contrary to the Word of God. Why world you get involved with bank robbers, murders, rapists, drug dealers, child molesters and the like? Why would you want to be named with such people and actions?

When a house is first built its not built of rotten wood, but sound wood; making it sound, beautiful and strong. But, unless cared for properly, it will deteriorate and become uninhabitable. Our body is God's creation and it should be kept                                                              as God created it; free of Satan's contamination, which make it uninhabitable for the Holy Spirit.

Again it is not speaking of marriage, because marriage in not a yoke. A yoke is a symbol of bondage or servitude and God did not institute the holy process of unity as a bondage to mankind. A yoke can never make you one, the best it can do is bring you close enough into the vicinity of another that it will make you appear to be doing the same thing as others that is yoked. And it is in this vicinity that many take it a step farther and become involved. Many declaring themselves believers are committing the acts of unbelievers. Bottom line; look at things Jesus tells us to do in our interaction with people; then look at things that are contrary to what Jesus said. Then, throw out all that don't agree with the teachings of Jesus Christ.

Joseph Haugabrook

## VENGEANCE WAS NOT ASSIGNED TO MAN

Romans 12:19-21

:19 Dearly beloved, avenge not yourselves, but rather give place unto wrath: for it is written, Vengeance is mine; I will repay, saith the Lord.

:20 Therefore if thine enemy hunger, feed him; if he thirst, give him drink; for in so doing thou shalt heap coals of fire on his head.

:21 Be not overcome of evil, but overcome evil with good.

The word to us is straight forward. There is a very good reason why revenge should never be a part of anyone's thoughts and actions. If I seek revenge or, get even, as we sometime refer to it; then I am letting someone else's words and deeds dictate my thinking and actions.

A word commonly used today, especially among the young is; respect. Give me respect. You better respect me. I did this or that to him or her because he or she didn't respect me. In this case the person clearly have in mind what he or she thinks respect is and when someone words or deeds doesn't align with what's in their minds they react; and that reaction will be, to do to the other person what they thought was done to them; hurt me and I'll hurt you worse. It is a case of an action being dictated by another action.

This is why Jesus it telling us not to get involved in revenge; because when we do we are trying to overcome evil with evil, and it's like adding one number to another, or gasoline to a fire. You can never reduce a number by adding to it, nor can you put out a fire by adding gasoline to it; both just grows greater. To put out a fire the thing fueling it must be removed. To reduce a number subtraction must take place. Jesus it telling us; good; will remove the things fueling evil. Good subtracts from evil; reducing it to zero;

You should not let someone else's words and deeds dictate your words and deeds. It's like you knowing the route to a town you are heading for, but refuse to take it.

## UNDERSTNDING REVELATION

To understand revelation it is important to understand how the language in Revelation extends, or covers the usage and meaning of words by mankind throughout the ages; from the beginning to the end of time.

Revelation is the same as the miracle on Pentecost when the Hebrews spoke in their native tongue; yet people from 19 other languages all heard the Hebrews in their own language. Example: a group of people; Chinese, Koreans, Africans, Spanish, etc; who only understand their own language; you speak to the group in English and each one hear and understand you in their native tongue. You are speaking English, but the Africans hear African being spoken. The Chinese hear Chinese being spoken and so on.
S
Revelation is given in such a way that the usage of

words, whether slang, proper English or what have you, is covered in an understandable way. We refer to transportation a lot different now than a century age; fast cars, super planes, missiles, etc. Weapons are different; earning a living, even enjoyment is different. But no matter how conditions, places and things change and words are used, Revelation is inclusive in it all. Revelation is given so it will be current to people and languages throughout time. It is important that facts be understood from the outset of studying revelation.

The way Revelation differs from the other books of the bible is: the Old Testament gives a record of God's plan for man on earth as shown with Adam and Eve in the Garden of Eden. It also shows Today's plan to redeem man from the curse of sin brought on by Adam's disobedient. It further shows the choosing of Abraham, and his seed, to show God's mercy, love and power to the world.

The new Testament; outlines how God culminated the plan of redeeming man from the curse of sin through the suffering and death of Jesus, who's; blood cleaned all mankind from sin; Matthew through John.

From Acts to Revelation mankind is given when, how, and what to do in keeping the teaching of Jesus. So, the New Testament gives how to live the life that is pleasing to Jesus. It demonstrates what happen when the Word, or teaching, of Jesus is obeyed. In short, it shows how Jesus desires us to live and the evils he try to prevent us from bringing on ourselves.

Revelation shows in detail the events occurring in Heaven and on earth as times progress. These events occur either because of acts of sin by mankind, or acts of righteousness. God desire is that we all will be obedient to His Word, but since we are not and since both sin and righteous acts has consequences commanded by God, these things take place, in Heaven and earth, as time progress. Because God knows what things man will do and what event will occur as a result, God is showing us what's going to take place.

God tells us that what is written in Revelation is faithful and true because` he knows that man is not going to repent from the destructive things he is doing. These destructive things are brought on by sin and God want us to know we can avoid being a part of it. He is urging us to take a good look at the terrible things sin is bringing upon man and flee from it, by coming to Him; our refuge.

Again, look at revelation's words and compare them to today words and descriptions of things. For example, when Revelation describes the sound of horses rushing to battle, think what a scary sound that must have been for the people of a different time. But note it's not the sound of the multitude of horses, but what it means; men fighting and killing, maiming and worse. So, it was the knowledge of war that was scary.

Today, it would be scary to hear the sound of many war planes, or missiles taking to the sky, knowing it meant war and retaliation. This is how Revelation is written so we can take the description of the events and associate it with our own time to give it meaning and to understand the dire warning from God.

261